MASTER KOREAN GRAMMAR
LEVEL 1

TOMI KOREAN

MP3 Audio Material Download

To enhance your learning experience, audio material is available for download. Visit https://tomikorean.com/audios/master-korean-grammar-level1. These audio resources are designed to complement your studies and improve your pronunciation and listening skills.

 Scan the QR code to visit the web page and access the audio files.

 PDF Additional Workbook Download

To download the workbook, please visit https://tomikorean.com/workbook-grammar-level1. The workbook provides extra exercises and practice materials to reinforce your understanding of Korean grammar concepts covered in the main textbook.

 Scan the QR code to visit the web page and access the pdf file.

For any inquiries or assistance, feel free to reach out to Tomi Korean at contact@tomikorean.com.

Copyright Notice

Introduction

Many Korean learners find learning the Korean language to be quite challenging due to its distinct structure, setting it apart from many other languages. Therefore, it is recommended to begin by familiarizing oneself with the basic grammar through learning and practice. We created this book to help you better understand basic Korean grammar. The following are the key aspects we focused on while developing this book:

- This Level 1 book, designed for absolute beginners, contains 47 fundamental grammar points and about 400 basic words, equivalent to half of TOPIK Level 1.

- Through this book, you can gradually grasp the complex rules of the Korean language by breaking them down into smaller units.

- The book is designed to help you internalize the rules through practice. In addition to basic exercises for each unit, you can strengthen your understanding with review tests at the end of each chapter and a workbook, available for free download from the website.

- The ultimate goal of mastering grammar is to use it proficiently in spoken and written Korean. This book is structured to facilitate the practical application of learned grammar in real-life situations.

Whether you've already acquired some knowledge of Korean or are new to it, this book will assist you in systematically organizing your learning. If you're a beginner, I believe this book will serve as the ideal starting point for your Korean learning journey, helping you build the essential foundation of the Korean language.

I sincerely hope that this book will be a valuable guide in your Korean learning journey.

January 2024,
Tomi Korean

How to use this book

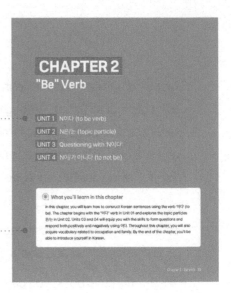

CHAPTER 2
"Be" Verb

UNIT 1 N이다 (to be verb)
UNIT 2 N은/는 (topic particle)
UNIT 3 Questioning with N이다
UNIT 4 N이/가 아니다 (to not be)

What you'll learn in this chapter
In this chapter, you will learn how to construct Korean sentences using the verb '이다' (to be). The chapter begins with the '이다' verb in Unit 01 and explores the topic particles 은는 in Unit 02. Units 03 and 04 will equip you with the skills to form questions and respond both positively and negatively using 이다. Throughout this chapter, you will also acquire vocabulary related to occupation and family. By the end of the chapter, you'll be able to introduce yourself in Korean.

Unit Overview

To make it easier understand essential grammar principles, the grammar topics have been systematically organized into units.

What to Expect in This Chapter

Preview the grammar concepts you will cover in this chapter.

Audio Resources

Listen to example sentences and exercises, and practice speaking using MP3 files downloaded from tomikorean.com.

Sample Sentences

Check out sentences made with the grammar learned in this unit.

Key Grammar Points

Quickly grasp the core grammar concepts with concise explanations and tables.

Vocabulary

See newly introduced vocabulary at a glance.

Practice Session

Strengthen your understanding of the grammar from each unit by solving exercises.

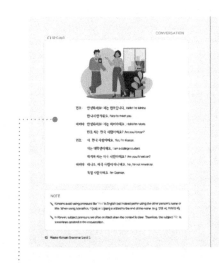

Chapter Recap

Summarize and reinforce the key grammar points covered in each chapter.

Real-Life Conversation

Explore how the learned grammar is applied in authentic, everyday conversations.

Review Test

Solidify your understanding of the essential grammar points through comprehensive review tests.

Vocabulary Checkpoint

Evaluate your mastery of new words introduced in each chapter through self-testing.

K-Culture Interlude

Finish each chapter with a short break, reading about Korean culture before moving to the next one.

Table of Contents

Learning Hangeul

What you'll learn in this chapter

In this chapter, you will learn how to read and write Hangeul, the script of the Korean language. Hangeul consists of 19 consonants and 21 vowels. We will go through each of them by type, so please follow along step by step. Due to its systematic structure, Hangeul is relatively easy to learn, so you will soon be able to read Korean with ease. Before delving into Korean grammar, familiarize yourself with Hangeul in this chapter!

❶ Hangeul

▶ Hangeul is composed of consonants and vowels.

▶ Hangeul consists of 40 letters (19 consonants + 21 vowels)[1].

▶ The five consonants (ㄱ, ㄴ, ㅁ, ㅅ, ㅇ) follow the shape of the speech organs[2] as they produce the sound while the rest are formed by adding strokes to these consonants.

ㄱ	ㄴ	ㄷ	ㄹ	ㅁ	ㅂ	ㅅ	ㅇ	ㅈ	ㅊ
ㅋ	ㅌ	ㅍ	ㅎ	ㄲ	ㄸ	ㅃ	ㅆ	ㅉ	

▶ The vowels are a combination of the symbols ' ㆍ ' (heaven) , 'ㅡ' (the earth) and 'ㅣ' (standing human). All vowels are composed of these three elements.[3]

ㅏ	ㅑ	ㅓ	ㅕ	ㅗ	ㅛ	ㅜ	ㅠ	ㅡ	ㅣ
ㅐ	ㅒ	ㅔ	ㅖ	ㅘ	ㅙ	ㅚ	ㅝ	ㅞ	ㅟ	ㅢ

❷ Composition of Korean Characters

▶ Hangeul characters are syllabic blocks consisting of consonants in the initial and final position, with a vowel in the medial position.

C V   ㄱ + ㅏ = 가

C/V   ㅅ + ㅗ = 소

C/V   ㅂ + ㅘ = 봐

C V/C   ㅎ + ㅏ + ㄴ = 한

C/V/C   ㅈ + ㅜ + ㄱ = 죽

C/V/C   ㅎ + ㅝ + ㄹ = 훨

---

[1] There are 14 basic consonants and 10 basic vowels. Among the letters below, those marked in green are the basic consonants and vowels.

[2] See page 22 for more details.

[3] For instance,
ㅣ + ㆍ → ㅏ
ㆍ + ㅣ → ㅓ
ㆍ + ㅡ → ㅗ
ㅏ + ㆍ → ㅑ

✓
Vertical vowels:
ㅏ, ㅑ, ㅓ, ㅕ, ㅣ
→ consonant on the left

Horizontal vowels:
ㅗ, ㅛ, ㅜ, ㅠ, ㅡ
→ consonant on top.

> You can download a workbook to practice writing Hangeul from https://tomikorean.com/workbook-grammar-level1/

Master Grammar By Practicing!

A Determine whether the given letter is a consonant or vowel.

ㄹ	→	(consonant / vowel)

1. ㅏ → (consonant / vowel)

2. ㅎ → (consonant / vowel)

3. ㅃ → (consonant / vowel)

4. ㅚ → (consonant / vowel)

5. ㅠ → (consonant / vowel)

B Determine whether the given combination of consonant and vowel is correct or incorrect.

사	→	(correct / incorrect)	ㅊ	→	(correct / incorrect)

1. ㅓㄷ → (correct / incorrect)

2. 수 → (correct / incorrect)

3. 패 → (correct / incorrect)

4. 바ㄷ → (correct / incorrect)

5. 쉰 → (correct / incorrect)

C Create a combination using the given consonants and vowels.

consonant: ㅅ, vowel: ㅜ, consonant: ㄹ	→	술

1. consonant: ㅁ, vowel: ㅒ → _____

2. consonant: ㅊ, vowel: ㅗ → _____

3. consonant: ㄴ, vowel: ㅏ, consonant: ㅁ → _____

4. consonant: ㅎ, vowel: ㅓ, consonant: ㄴ → _____

5. consonant: ㅈ, vowel: ㅗ, consonant: ㄱ → _____

UNIT 2 | 모음 1: Basic Vowels

 00-02H.mp3

❶ Basic Vowels

▶ There are 21 vowels in Hangeul, including 10 basic vowels and 11 complex vowels. In this unit, focus on learning the 10 basic vowels first.

▶ Vowels are written from top to bottom, and from left to right.

Letter	Name	Romanization	Sounds like
ㅏ	아	[a]	father
ㅑ	야	[ya]	yard
ㅓ	어	[eo]	up
ㅕ	여	[yeo]	yummy
ㅗ	오	[o]	old
ㅛ	요	[yo]	yoga
ㅜ	우	[u]	cool
ㅠ	유	[yu]	you
ㅡ	으	[eu]	good, uh
ㅣ	이	[i]	tree

 A vowel forms a syllable. If there's no consonant at the start of a syllabic block, 'ㅇ' is used as a silent filler. Thus, 'ㅇ|' is pronounced the same as the vowel 'ㅣ'.

ㅇ + ㅏ → 아 [a]
ㅇ + ㅗ → 오 [o]

The Romanization of this book follows Revised Romanization of Korean, the official Korean language romanization system, developed by the National Academy of the Korean Language.

❷ Words with Basic Vowels

아이 [a·i]

child

오이 [o·i]

cucumber

여우 [yeo·u]

fox

우유 [u·yu]

milk

이 [i]

tooth

Master Grammar By Practicing!

🎧 00-02P.mp3

A Listen to the audio and choose the correct answer.

(아 / <u>어</u> / 우)

1. (오 / 유 / 이)
2. (어 / 야 / 으)
3. (요 / 오 / 우)
4. (으 / 이 / 여)
5. (여 / 요 / 유)

B Listen to the audio and choose the correct answer.

(<u>우유</u> / 오이)

1. (여우 / 아이)
2. (이 / 우유)
3. (아이 / 오이)
4. (여우 / 우유)

C Listen to the audio and write the answer.

<u>아이</u>

1. _____
2. _____
3. _____
4. _____

UNIT 3 | 자음 1: Basic Consonants

00-03H.mp3

❶ Basic Consonants

▶ There are 19 consonants in Hangeul, including 14 basic consonants and 5 double consonants. In this unit, focus on learning the 14 basic consonants first.

Letter	Name[1]	Romanization Initial	Romanization final[3]	Sounds like	Syllable with ㅏ
ㄱ	기역	[g]	[k]	go	가 [ga]
ㄴ	니은		[n]	no	나 [na]
ㄷ	디귿	[d]	[t]	study	다 [da]
ㄹ	리을	[r], [l][2]	[l]	lemon	라 [la]
ㅁ	미음		[m]	map	마 [ma]
ㅂ	비읍	[b]	[p]	busy	바 [ba]
ㅅ	시옷	[s]	[t]	slow	사 [sa]
ㅇ	이응	–	[ng]	ring	아 [a]
ㅈ[4]	지읒	[j]	[t]	jar	자 [ja]
ㅊ[4]	치읓	[ch]	[t]	child	차 [cha]
ㅋ	키읔		[k]	Korea	카 [ka]
ㅌ	티읕		[t]	teeth	타 [ta]
ㅍ	피읖		[p]	power	파 [pa]
ㅎ	히읗	[h]	[t]	hat	하 [ha]

✓ Consonants have no sound on their own; therefore, consonants must be used in combination with vowels to complete a syllable.

ㅁ + ㅏ → 마 [ma]
ㄷ + ㅗ → 도 [do]

[1] You don't need to memorize the names of consonants. Getting used to their sounds is more important.

[2] Between two vowels, it is pronounced as [r], as in 소리 [sori]. In other cases, it is pronounced as [l], as in 말 [mal]

[3] See page 20 for information about 'Final Consonant'.

[4] Depending on fonts, ㅈ can be written as ㅈ, and ㅊ can be written as ㅊ.

❷ Words with One Basic Consonant and One Basic Vowel

기차 [gi·cha]
train

나무 [na·mu]
tree

바나나 [ba·na·na]
banana

치마 [chi·ma]
skirt

커피 [keo·pi]
coffee

Master Grammar By Practicing!

🎧 00-03P.mp3

A Listen to the audio and choose the correct answer.

(가 / 마 / <u>나</u>)

1. (바 / 아 / 자)
2. (라 / 하 / 타)
3. (파 / 다 / 사)
4. (사 / 차 / 카)
5. (자 / 가 / 다)

B Listen to the audio and choose the correct answer.

(<u>아기</u> / 커피)

1. (기차 / 모자)
2. (지도 / 하나)
3. (버스 / 나무)
4. (가구 / 비누)
5. (치마 / 포도)

C Listen to the audio and write the answer.

<u>나무</u>

1. _____
2. _____
3. _____
4. _____

UNIT 4 모음 2: Complex Vowels

 00-04H.mp3

❶ Complex Vowels

▶ The following are 11 complex vowels composed of the 10 basic vowels.

Letter	Name	Romanization	Sounds like
ㅐ	애	[ae]	sad
ㅒ	얘	[yae]	yes
ㅔ	에	[e]	bed, pet
ㅖ	예	[ye]	yes
ㅘ	와	[wa]	swan
ㅙ	왜	[wae]	wet
ㅚ	외	[oe]	wet
ㅝ	워	[wo]	wonderful
ㅞ	웨	[we]	wet
ㅟ	위	[wi]	we
ㅢ	의	[ui]	uh-ee

✓
ㅐ and ㅔ
They are often not distinguished in speech despite their different pronunciation. The same goes for ㅙ, ㅚ, and ㅞ.

However, be cautious when writing, as the spelling affects the meaning in words and sentences.

✓
Syllables
ㄷ + ㅟ → 뒤 [dwi]
ㄱ + ㅘ → 과 [gwa]

❷ Words with Complex Vowels

개 [gae]

dog

노래 [no·rae]

song

사과 [sa·gwa]

apple

의사 [ui·sa]

doctor

테니스 [te·ni·seu]

tennis

Master Grammar By Practicing!

🎧 00-04P.mp3

A Listen to the audio and choose the correct answer.

(워 / 와 / <u>왜</u>)

1. (애 / 의 / 외)
2. (배 / 봐 / 뷔)
3. (과 / 궤 / 귀)
4. (뇌 / 네 / 놔)
5. (쥐 / 줘 / 쟤)

B Listen to the audio and choose the correct answer.

(뇌 / <u>의사</u>)

1. (개 / 새)
2. (의자 / 화가)
3. (사과 / 가게)
4. (카메라 / 개구리)
5. (노래 / 시계)

C Listen to the audio and write the answer.

<u>의사</u>

1. _____
2. _____
3. _____
4. _____

UNIT 5 | 자음 2: Double Consonants

🎧 00-05H.mp3

❶ Double Consonants

▶ The following 5 double consonants are formed by doubling the basic consonants.

Letter	Name	Romanization	Sounds like
ㄲ	쌍기역	[kk]	school
ㄸ	쌍디귿	[tt]	steal
ㅃ	쌍비읍	[pp]	spoon
ㅆ	쌍시옷	[ss]	sit
ㅉ	쌍지읒	[jj]	judge

✅ Syllables
ㄸ + ㅗ → 또 [tto]
ㅆ + ㅐ → 쌔 [ssae]

Korean consonants can be classified as neutral, aspirated, and tensed depending on syllable formation. The neutral has no strong air release, while the aspirated has a forceful release, and the tensed is pronounced with tense tongue muscles.

	Letter					Syllable with ㅏ				
Neutral	ㄱ	ㄷ	ㅂ	ㅅ	ㅈ	가[ga]	다[da]	바[ba]	사[sa]	자[ja]
Aspirated	ㅋ	ㅌ	ㅍ		ㅊ	카[ka]	타[ta]	파[pa]		차[cha]
Tensed	ㄲ	ㄸ	ㅃ	ㅆ	ㅉ	까[kka]	따[tta]	빠[ppa]	싸[ssa]	짜[jja]

❷ Words with Double Consonants

싸다 [ssa·da]
to be cheap

쓰다 [sseu·da]
to write

아빠 [a·ppa]
dad

예쁘다 [ye·ppeu·da]
to be pretty

토끼 [to·kki]
rabbit

Master Grammar By Practicing!

🎧 00-05P.mp3

A Listen to the audio and choose the correct answer.

(<u>까</u> / 빠 / 싸)

1. (뿌 / 쭈 / 꾸)
2. (쪼 / 쏘 / 뽀)
3. (끼 / 삐 / 찌)
4. (쓰 / 끄 / 뜨)
5. (빼 / 때 / 쌔)

B Listen to the audio and choose the correct answer.

(<u>아빠</u> / 꼬리)

1. (짜다 / 쓰다)
2. (토끼 / 뿌리)
3. (비싸다 / 싸다)
4. (예쁘다 / 찌르다)
5. (끄다 / 씨)

C Listen to the audio and write the answer.

<u>쓰다</u>

1. _____
2. _____
3. _____
4. _____

UNIT 6 | 받침: Final Consonants

🎧 00-06H.mp3

❶ Final Consonants

▶ Final consonants are used in the final position of a syllabic block.

▶ All consonants except for ㄸ, ㅃ, ㅉ can be used as final consonants.

▶ Some of them are not pronounced as they are. The pronunciation changes to one of the following 7 consonant sounds.

✓ Syllables
ㅁ + ㅗ + ㅁ → 몸 [mom]
ㅂ + ㅏ + ㅇ → 방 [bang]
ㅊ + ㅐ + ㄱ → 책 [chaek]

Final Consonant	Romanization	Example
ㄱ, ㅋ, ㄲ	[k]	책, 먹다, 부엌, 밖
ㄴ	[n]	문, 손, 돈, 편지
ㄷ, ㅅ, ㅈ ㅊ, ㅌ, ㅎ, ㅆ	[t]	듣다, 옷, 낮, 꽃, 끝, 파랗다, 있다
ㄹ	[l]	말, 술, 올해
ㅁ	[m]	몸, 여름, 김치
ㅂ, ㅍ	[p]	밥, 잡다, 잎, 덮다
ㅇ	[ng]	강, 방, 공부, 강아지

❷ Double Final Consonants

▶ ㄶ, ㄼ, ㅄ → Pronunciation follows the first consonant of the double final consonant.

앉다 [안따: an·tta]   많다 [만타: man·ta]   여덟 [여덜: yeo·deol]   값 [갑: gap]

▶ ㄺ, ㄻ → Pronunciation follows the second consonant of the double final consonant.

닭 [닥: dak]   밝다 [박따: bak·tta]   삶 [삼: sam]   젊다 [점따: jeom·tta]

❸ Words with Final Consonants

꽃 [kkot]
flower

듣다 [deut·tta]
to listen

밥 [bap]
rice

옷 [ot]
clothes

책 [chaek]
book

Master Grammar By Practicing!

🎧 00-06P.mp3

A Listen to the audio and choose the correct answer.

(<u>상</u> / 삭 / 삽)

1. (김 / 길 / 긴)
2. (밥 / 방 / 박)
3. (꽃 / 꽁 / 꼭)
4. (말 / 망 / 만)
5. (술 / 숲 / 숭)

B Listen to the audio and choose the correct answer.

(<u>옷</u> / 낮)

1. (꽃 / 못)
2. (먹다 / 듣다)
3. (산 / 밥)
4. (몸 / 책)
5. (강 / 손)

C Listen to the audio and write the answer.

밥

1. _____
2. _____
3. _____
4. _____

The Legacy of King Sejong: The Birth of Hangeul

The Korean alphabet, known as Hangeul, was invented in 1443 by 세종대왕 (King Sejong), the fourth monarch of Joseon, and the scholars of 집현전 (Jiphyeonjeon: The Academy of Worthies). Before the introduction Hangeul, Korean was written using Chinese characters, posing a significant challenge for ordinary people to learn. King Sejong recognized the need for a writing system that was accessible to all, regardless of social status or education.

Hangeul is celebrated for its scientific and logical design. Its characters are formed by combining consonants and vowels into syllabic blocks, providing a phonetic representation of the spoken language. This innovation made learning to read and write more accessible to the Korean people.

The Ingenious Creation of Hangeul

The consonants (자음) in Hangeul were designed to represent the shape and articulation of the speech organs during their pronunciation. King Sejong classified sounds into basic categories, each reflected in the visual form of the corresponding consonant.
For example: 'ㄴ' (n) mirrors the tip of the tongue against the upper front teeth. And 'ㅁ' (m) imitates closed lips, representing a nasal sound.

The vowels (모음) are a combination of three elemental symbols — ' • ' representing heaven, ' — ' symbolizing the earth, and ' ㅣ ' representing a standing human being. All vowels are composed of these three elements.

King Sejong's meticulous approach ensured that Hangeul not only accurately represented sounds but also provided a visual connection to the spoken language. The result is a script that embodies the spirit of linguistic democracy, enabling everyone to express themselves through the beauty and simplicity of Hangeul.

CHAPTER 1
Characteristics of Korean

What you'll learn in this chapter

The Korean language differs significantly from many other languages, potentially making it challenging to learn. Therefore, it is recommended to familiarize yourself with its key features before you get started with learning Korean. This chapter focuses on the general characteristics of Korean, so there's no need to worry if you don't grasp all the details at once. All grammar points will be systematically covered in this book, allowing you to learn them step by step.

UNIT 1 Korean Sentence Structure

🎧 01-01G.mp3

❶ Word Order in Korean

▶ While English follows the SVO order (subject + verb + object),
Korean follows the SOV order (subject + object + verb/predicate).

▶ Korean verbs always come at the end of the sentence.

<u>Jenny</u> <u>buys</u> <u>a book</u>.
subject verb   object

제니가 책을 사요.
subject object verb

▶ If there is no object, the sentence consists of 'subject + verb'.

<u>Daniel</u> <u>sleeps</u>.
subject   verb

다니엘이 자요.
subject verb

❷ Particles

▶ Korean has many particles which are attached to the end of a noun.

▶ Particles indicate what role the noun plays in the sentence.

> Jenny buys a book at the bookstore.
>
> ### 제니 가 서점 에서 책 을 사요.
> subject   adverbial   object

 The particle 이 or 가 is used after the subject, 을 or 를 after the object. There are also adverbial particles indicating time or location, such as 에, 에서, and 부터.

You will learn these essential Korean particles one by one in the upcoming lessons.

❸ Position of Words

▶ The position of subjects, objects, and adverbials can change based on the speaker's intention.[1]

▶ This flexibility exists because the particles still indicate the roles of words in the sentence.

제니가 서점에서 책을 사요.　　제니가 책을 서점에서 사요.
서점에서 제니가 책을 사요.　　서점에서 책을 제니가 사요.
책을 제니가 서점에서 사요.　　책을 서점에서 제니가 사요.

→ All of these sentences mean 'Jenny buys a book at the bookstore'.

[1] However, the verbs always come at the end of the sentence!

Master Grammar By Practicing!

🎧 01-01P.mp3

A Choose the verb/predicate in the sentences.

제니가 / 빵을 / 먹어요.	Jenny eats bread.

1. 민호가 / 와요.   Minho comes.
2. 엄마가 / 책을 / 읽어요.   My mom reads a book.
3. 다니엘이 / 집에 / 가요.   Daniel goes home.
4. 유나가 / 공부해요.   Yuna studies.
5. 아빠가 / 사과를 / 사요.   My dad buys apples.

B Find and mark the subject particle '이' or '가' in the sentences.

제니가 빵을 먹어요.	Jenny eats bread.

1. 민호가 책을 읽어요.   Minho reads a book.
2. 다니엘이 공부해요.   Daniel studies.
3. 유나가 와요.   Yuna comes.
4. 마이클이 가방을 사요.   Michael buys a bag.
5. 엄마가 사과를 먹어요.   My mom eats an apple.

C Find and mark the object particle '을' or '를' in the sentences.

제니가 빵을 먹어요.	Jenny eats bread.

1. 민호가 밥을 먹어요.   Minho eats rice.
2. 다니엘이 한국어를 공부해요.   Daniel studies Korean.
3. 엄마가 BTS를 좋아해요.   My mom likes BTS.
4. 유나가 책을 읽어요.   Yuna reads a book.
5. 마이클이 사과를 사요.   Michael buys apples.

🎧 01-02G.mp3

❶ Korean Verbs and Adjectives

▶ Korean verbs and adjectives have the same basic form (infinitive), ending with -다.

먹다[1] [meok·tta] to eat   사다 [sa·da] to buy

일하다 [il·ha·da] to work   작다[1] [jak·tta] to be small

예쁘다 [ye·ppeu·da] to be pretty   따뜻하다 [tta·tteut·ta·da] to be warm

[1] If there is a consonant in front of 다, 다 [da] is pronounced as [tta].

❷ Conjugation of Verbs and Adjectives

▶ Both Korean verbs and adjectives use various conjugations to indicate tense, politeness level, and formality.

▶ The form of verbs and adjectives doesn't change based on the gender or number of the subject.[2]

▶ Like many languages, Korean has irregular verbs that don't follow the standard conjugation patterns.

[2] It remains the same whether the subject is singular or plural, male or female.

학생이 공부해요.
A student studies.
많은 학생이 공부해요.
Many students study.

Examples in Basic Form:

You will learn more detailed conjugation in Chapter 6.

Examples of Conjugation:

먹습니다: eat
→ 먹 + 습니다 (formal polite form in the present tense)

먹었어요: ate
→ 먹 + 었 (past tense) + 어요 (informal polite form)

먹으셨어: ate
→ 먹 + 으시 (honorific) + 었 (past tense) + 어 (casual form)

Master Grammar By Practicing!

🎧 01-02P.mp3

A Find and mark the word ending '다' in the basic form of the verbs and adjectives.

| to go | → | 가다 | to be small | → | 작다 |

1. to read → 읽다
2. to be warm → 따뜻하다
3. to work → 일하다
4. to be pretty → 예쁘다
5. to eat → 먹다

B Find and write the word stem in the basic forms of the verbs and adjectives.

| 가다 to go → 가 | 예쁘다 to be pretty → 예쁘 |

1. 먹다 to eat → _____
2. 마시다 to drink → _____
3. 사다 to buy → _____
4. 작다 to be small → _____
5. 따뜻하다 to be warm → _____

C From the two options, choose the form in which the verb or adjective is conjugated.

| to come | → | (오다 / 오셨어요) |

1. to eat → (먹었습니다 / 먹다)
2. to be small → (작으셨어 / 작다)
3. to be warm → (따뜻하다 / 따뜻했어요)
4. to drink → (마시세요 / 마시다)
5. to sleep → (자다 / 잡니다)

 01-03G.mp3

❶ Korean Speech Style

▶ The Korean language officially has seven different speech styles.

▶ Speech styles depend on the relationship between the speakers.

▶ They can be categorized into three main forms commonly used: formal polite, informal polite and casual

Korean speech style is divided into two main categories:

1. 존댓말 [jon·daet·mal]: Polite speech (formal polite and informal polite form)
2. 반말 [ban·mal]: Casual speech (casual form)

반말 literally means 'half speech', and it's shorter than 존댓말.

❷ Formal Polite Form: –(스)ㅂ니다 [sseum·ni·da]

▶ The formal polite form is mainly used in formal or public situations:
→ official announcements, news broadcasts, school or work presentations, job interviews, customer interactions, and in the military

가다 to go → 갑니다   먹다 to go → 먹습니다

❸ Informal Polite Form: –아/어요 [a/eo·yo]

▶ The informal polite form is less formal but still polite.

▶ It is the most commonly used for almost all situations where politeness is expected in daily life:
→ among family members, friends, acquaintances, colleagues, people older than you, and strangers

가다 to go → 가요   먹다 to go → 먹어요

You will learn more detailed conjugation in Chapter 6.

❹ Casual Form: –아/어 [a/eo]

▶ The casual form is used where politeness of formality is not required:
→ among intimate friends, family members, or with people with whom you have agreed to use '반말 (casual speech)'

가다 to go → 가   먹다 to go → 먹어

⚠ It is considered rude to use the casual form with someone you are meeting for the first time or with whom you are not very close.

Master Grammar By Practicing!

🎧 01-03P.mp3

A Choose the option that is conjugated into a formal polite form.

읽다 to read	→	(읽습니다 / 읽어요)

1. 마시다 to drink → (마셔 / 마십니다)
2. 좋다 to be good → (좋습니다 / 좋아요)
3. 일하다 to work → (일합니다 / 일해)
4. 보다 to see → (봐 / 봅니다)
5. 따뜻하다 to be warm → (따뜻해요 / 따뜻합니다)

B Choose the option that is conjugated into an informal polite form.

좋아하다 to like	→	(좋아해 / 좋아해요)

1. 먹다 to eat → (먹습니다 / 먹어요)
2. 따뜻하다 to be warm → (따뜻해 / 따뜻해요)
3. 읽다 to read → (읽어요 / 읽습니다)
4. 예쁘다 to be pretty → (예뻐요 / 예뻐)
5. 사다 to buy → (삽니다 / 사요)

C Choose the option that is conjugated into a casual form.

보다 to see	→	(봐 / 봐요)

1. 작다 to be small → (작아 / 작아요)
2. 마시다 to drink → (마셔 / 마십니다)
3. 사다 to buy → (삽니다 / 사)
4. 좋다 to be good → (좋아요 / 좋아)
5. 예쁘다 to be pretty → (예뻐 / 예쁩니다)

🎧 01-04G.mp3

In Korean, numbers can be expressed in two ways. One uses Sino-Korean numbers, which originate from Chinese characters, and the other uses native Korean numbers. Each type of number is used in different situations.

1 Sino-Korean Numbers

▶ Sino-Korean numbers are used to express things such as telephone numbers, prices, height, weight, address, years, months, minutes, and seconds.

0	공 [gong] or 영 [yeong]						
1	일 [il]	11	십일 [si·bil]	21	이십일 [i·si·bil]	...	...
2	이 [i]	12	십이 [si·bi]	...	...	200	이백 [i·baek]
3	삼 [sam]	13	십삼 [sip·sam]	30	삼십 [sam·sip]	300	삼백 [sam·baek]
4	사 [sa]	14	십사 [sip·sa]	40	사십 [sa·sip]	400	사백 [sa·baek]
5	오 [o]	15	십오 [si·bo]	50	오십 [o·sip]	500	오백 [o·baek]
6	육 [yuk]	16	십육 [sip·yuk]	60	육십 [yuk·sip]	...	...
7	칠 [chil]	17	십칠 [sip·chil]	70	칠십 [chil·sip]	1,000	천[1] [cheon]
8	팔 [pal]	18	십팔 [si·pal]	80	팔십 [pal·sip]	10,000	만[1] [man]
9	구 [gu]	19	십구 [sip·gu]	90	구십 [gu·sip]	100,000	십만 [sip·man]
10	십[1] [sip]	20	이십 [i·sip]	100	백[1] [baek]	1,000,000	백만 [baek·man]

[1] 10 - 십 (not 일십),
100 - 백 (not 일백)
1,000 - 천 (not 일천)
10,000 - 만 (not 일만)

010-2416-8741 → 공일공 이사일육 팔칠사일[2]
No. 172 → 백칠십이 번
164 cm → 백육십사 센티미터
53,000 Won → 오만 삼천 원

[2] The '0' in a phone number is said to be 공 (not 영).

▶ In Korean, large numbers are read in units of 10,000 (만), not 1,000 (천) There should be a space after 만, and the remaining part of the number follows.

210,000	→	21 / 0000	→	이십일만
125,600	→	12 / 5600	→	십이만 오천육백
3,416,587	→	341 / 6587	→	삼백사십일만 육천오백팔십칠

❷ Native Korean Numbers

▶ Native Korean numbers are used to express hours and to count things or people. They are typically used along with appropriate counters.

1	하나 [ha·na]	11	열하나 [yeol·ha·na]	21	스물하나 [seu·mul·ha·na]	26	스물여섯	
2	둘 [dul]	12	열둘 [yeol·dul]	...	...	41	마흔하나	
3	셋 [set]	13	열셋 [yeol·set]	30	서른 [seo·reun]	38	서른여덟	
4	넷 [net]	14	열넷 [yeol·net]	40	마흔 [ma·heun]	32	서른둘	
5	다섯 [da·seot]	15	열다섯 [yeol·da·seot]	50	쉰 [swin]			
6	여섯 [yeo·seot]	16	열여섯 [yeol·yeo·seot]	60	예순 [ye·sun]			
7	일곱 [il·gop]	17	열일곱 [yeol·il·gop]	70	일흔 [il·heun]			
8	여덟 [yeo·deol]	18	열여덟 [yeol·yeo·deol]	80	여든 [yeo·deun]			
9	아홉 [a·hop]	19	열아홉 [yeol·a·hop]	90	아흔 [a·heun]			
10	열 [yeol]	20	스물 [seu·mul]	100	백 [baek]			

✓ You will learn how to count numbers in Chapter 8.

Master Grammar By Practicing!

PRACTICE

🎧 01-04P.mp3

A Write the given numbers as a Sino-Korean number.

381	→	삼백팔십일	125,300	→	십이만 오천삼백

1. 74 → _____
2. 82,000 → _____
3. 276 → _____
4. 541,230 → _____

B Write the given numbers as a native Korean number.

24	→	스물넷	45	→	마흔다섯

1. 17 → _____
2. 29 → _____
3. 36 → _____
4. 41 → _____

Korean Greetings You Need To Know

To kick off your journey of learning Korean, why not begin by learning how to say hello in Korean? In this page, you will explore the most basic and polite Korean greetings used when meeting or leaving someone, as well as when expressing gratitude or apology.

When Meeting
In Korean, initiating a conversation often starts with the standard greeting, "안녕하세요?". For formal or official encounters, "안녕하십니까?" adds an extra layer of politeness, demonstrating respect for the other person.

> 안녕하세요? [an·nyeong·ha·se·yo]

> 안녕하십니까? [an·nyeong·ha·sim·ni·kka]

When Saying Goodbye
When saying goodbye to someone who is leaving, it's customary to use the phrase "안녕히 가세요" emphasizing a safe journey. Conversely, when you're the one leaving, "안녕히 계세요" wishes the staying person well and encourages them to take care.

> 안녕히 가세요. [an·nyeong·hi ga·se·yo]

> 안녕히 계세요. [an·nyeong·hi gye·se·yo]

When Expressing Gratitude
Gratitude is a universal language, and in Korean, you can express it through "감사합니다" or "고맙습니다".

> 고맙습니다. [go·map·sseum·ni·da]

> 감사합니다. [gam·sa·ham·ni·da]

When Apologizing
"죄송합니다" and "미안합니다" convey apologies with a genuine tone. "죄송합니다." conveys a more formal nuance than "미안합니다." dose.

> 죄송합니다. [joe·song·ham·ni·da]

> 미안합니다. [mi·an·ham·ni·da]

CHAPTER 2
"Be" Verb

UNIT 1 N이다 (to be verb)

UNIT 2 N은/는 (topic particle)

UNIT 3 Questioning with 'N이다'

UNIT 4 N이/가 아니다 (to not be)

🎯 What you'll learn in this chapter

In this chapter, you will learn how to construct Korean sentences using the verb '이다' (to be). The chapter begins with the '이다' verb in Unit 01 and explores the topic particles 은/는 in Unit 02. Units 03 and 04 will equip you with the skills to form questions and respond both positively and negatively using '이다'. Throughout this chapter, you will also acquire vocabulary related to occupation and family. By the end of the chapter, you'll be able to introduce yourself in Korean.

UNIT 1 | N이다 (to be verb)

 02-01G.mp3

> 저는 제니예요.
> I am Jenny.

> 저는 학생이에요.
> I am a student.

❶ N이다 [i·da]: to be N

▶ 이다 is used to connect the subject of a sentence with a predicate.

▶ It's equivalent to the English verb 'to be'.

▶ It's attached to the end of a noun.

✔
Differences with English
Korean 'be' verbs <u>do not</u> change based on the gender or singular/plural form of the subject.

❷ Rules (informal polite form)

If the noun ends with a consonant,	If the noun ends with a vowel,
Noun + 이에요	**Noun + 예요**
선생님 + 이에요	**가수 + 예요**

❸ Basic Conjugation

	Consonant-Ending Nouns	Vowel-Ending Nouns
Formal Polite	**N입니다** [im·ni·da] 선생님입니다 | 가수입니다	
Informal Polite	**N이에요** [i·e·yo] 선생님이에요	**N예요** [ye·yo] 가수예요
Casual	**N이야** [i·ya] 선생님이야	**N야** [ya] 가수야

→ The informal polite form is the most commonly used in everyday conversation.

저는 선생님이에요.   I'm a teacher.

저는 가수예요.   I'm a singer.

WORDS
저 [jeo] I (polite)
가수 [ga·su] singer
학생 [hak·saeng] student
선생님 [seon·saeng·nim] teacher

Master Grammar By Practicing!

 02-01P.mp3

A Choose the correct option to match the noun in an informal polite style.

저는 가수(예요 / 이에요).	I am a singer.

1. 저는 학생(예요 / 이에요).　　　 I am a student.
2. 저는 다니엘(예요 / 이에요).　　 I am Daniel.
3. 저는 한국 사람(예요 / 이에요).　 I am Korean.
4. 저는 의사(예요 / 이에요).　　　 I am a doctor.

B Complete the sentences in three different styles.

I'm a teacher.	선생님입니다 / 이에요 / 이야.

1. I'm a doctor.　 의사_____ / _____ / _____
2. I'm a student.　 학생_____ / _____ / _____
3. I'm a singer.　 가수_____ / _____ / _____
4. I'm American.　 미국 사람_____ / _____ / _____

C Change the underlined verb into a correct form, in case it is incorrect.

저는 의사이에요.	(correct / incorrect → 예요)

1. 저는 선생님니다.　　 (correct / incorrect → 　　　)
2. 저는 미국 사람이에요.　 (correct / incorrect → 　　　)
3. 저는 가수이에요.　　 (correct / incorrect → 　　　)
4. 저는 학생예요.　　 (correct / incorrect → 　　　)

WORDS

한국 [han·guk] Korea　　　　사람 [sa·ram] person
의사 [ui·sa] doctor　　　　　미국 [mi·guk] USA

🎧 02-02G.mp3

동생은 학생이에요.　　어머니는 선생님이에요.
My brother/sister is a student.　My mother is a teacher.

❶ N은/는 [eun/neun] : Topic Particle

▶ 은/는 is a particle used to indicate the topic of a sentence.

▶ It comes right after the noun and clarifies what the sentence is about.

▶ Hence, the noun serves as the primary subject in the sentence.

❷ Rules

If the noun ends with a consonant,	If the noun ends with a vowel,
Noun + 은	**Noun + 는**
동생 + 은	어머니 + 는

나[1]는 학생이야.　　　　　I am a student.
오빠는 의사예요.　　　　　My older brother is a doctor.
형은 가수예요.　　　　　　My older brother is a singer.

[1]나 [na] is a informal term for 'I,' typically used in casual speech, as opposed to 저 [jeo] in polite speech.

Differences with English
In Korean, possessive pronouns like 'my' are often omitted, unlike in English. For example, '엄마' can mean 'my mom' without using a possessive pronoun.

How to refer siblings in Korean

In Korea, how you refer siblings depends on your gender and their age:
As a girl: older brothers are called 오빠[o·ppa], older sisters are called 언니[eon·ni].
As a boy: older brothers are called 형[hyeong], older sisters are called 누나[nu·na].

Younger siblings are always 동생[dong·saeng], but you can specify 남동생 [nam·dong·saeng] for a younger brother and 여동생[yeo·dong·saeng] for a younger sister.

WORDS

동생 [dong·saeng] younger brother/sister　　　어머니 [eo·meo·ni] mother　　　나[na] I (casual)
오빠 [o·ppa] older brother for girls　　　　　형 [hyeong] older brother for boys

Master Grammar By Practicing!

🎧 02-02P.mp3

A Choose the correct topic particle.

엄마(은 / 는) 선생님이에요.	My mom is a teacher.

1. 나(은 / 는) 학생이야.   I am a student.
2. 동생(은 / 는) 가수예요.   My brother/sister is a singer.
3. 아버지(은 / 는) 선생님입니다.   My father is a teacher.
4. 저(은 / 는) 독일 사람이에요.   I am German.

B Correct the topic particle, in case it is incorrect.

My brother/sister is a student.	동생<u>는</u> 학생이에요.	(correct / incorrect → 은)

1. My dad is a teacher.   아빠<u>은</u> 선생님이에요.   (correct / incorrect →   )
2. My older sister is a doctor.   누나<u>는</u> 의사예요.   (correct / incorrect →   )
3. My older brother is a singer.   오빠<u>은</u> 가수야.   (correct / incorrect →   )
4. My older sister is Korean.   언니<u>은</u> 한국 사람입니다.   (correct / incorrect →   )

C Choose the correct topic particle and arrange the sentences correctly.

엄마 이에요 선생님	(은 / 는) → <u>엄마는 선생님이에요.</u>

1. 이야   학생   동생   (은 / 는) → _____
2. 미국 사람   입니다   저   (은 / 는) → _____
3. 이에요   아버지   선생님   (은 / 는) → _____
4. 의사   야   엄마   (은 / 는) → _____

WORDS

엄마 [eom·ma] mom   아버지 [a·beo·ji] father   독일 [do·gil] Germany
아빠 [a·ppa] dad   누나 [nu·na] older sister for boys   언니 [eon·ni] older sister for girls

🎧 02-03G.mp3

> **오빠는 학생이에요?**
> Is your older brother a student?

> **네, 오빠는 학생이에요.**
> Yes, my older brother is a student.

❶ Question Form of 이다

▶ The question form in Korean is the same as the descriptive form.
  이에요 → 이에요? (informal polite)   이야 → 이야? (casual)

▶ In case of formal expression, 입니다 is changed to 입니까?

▶ Interrogative sentences typically end with a rising intonation.

❷ Basic Conjugation

	Consonant-Ending Nouns	Vowel-Ending Nouns
Formal Polite	**N입니까?** [im·ni·kka] 선생님입니까? ǀ 가수입니까?	
Informal Polite	**N이에요?** [i·e·yo] 선생님이에요?	**N예요?** [ye·yo] 가수예요?
Casual	**N이야?** [i·ya] 선생님이야?	**N야?** [ya] 가수야?

→ The informal polite form is the most commonly used in everyday conversation.

❸ Yes/No in Korean

	Yes	No
Polite	네 [ne] or 예 [ye]	아니요 [a·ni·yo]
Casual	응 [eung] (어 [eo]: colloquial)	아니 [a·ni]

Q: 엄마는 선생님이에요?　　　Is your mom a teacher?

A: 네, 선생님이에요.　　　　　Yes, she's a teacher.

A: 아니요, 가수예요.　　　　　No, she's a singer.

Master Grammar By Practicing!

🎧 02-03P.mp3

A Choose the correct question form of '이다'.

> 동생은 학생(예요 / 이에요)?   Is your brother/sister a student?

1. 언니는 의사(예요 / 이에요)?   Is your older sister a doctor?
2. 형은 회사원(예요 / 이에요)?   Is your older brother an office worker?
3. 오빠는 가수(야 / 이야)?   Is your older brother a singer?
4. 누나는 대학생(야 / 이야)?   Is your older sister a college student?

B Write the correct answer in polite style, choosing between '네(yes)' and '아니요(no)'.

> 엄마는 의사예요? (엄마=의사) → 네.   엄마는 의사예요? (엄마=선생님) → 아니요.

1. 형은 가수입니까? (형=학생)   → _____
2. 언니는 대학생이에요? (언니=대학생) → _____
3. 누나는 배우입니까? (누나=학생)   → _____
4. 아버지는 선생님이에요? (아버지=의사) → _____

C Write the correct answer in casual style, choosing between '응(yes)' and '아니(no)'.

> 오빠는 가수야? (오빠=가수) → 응.   오빠는 가수야? (오빠=배우) → 아니.

1. 동생은 대학생이야? (동생=의사)   → _____
2. 제니는 한국 사람이야? (제니=미국 사람) → _____
3. 누나는 의사야? (누나=의사)   → _____
4. 형은 배우야? (형=배우)   → _____

WORDS

회사원 [hoe·sa·won] office worker   **대학생** [dae·hak·saeng] college student

배우 [bae·u] actor, actress

UNIT 4 | N이/가 아니다 (to not be)

> 엄마는 선생님이 아니에요.
> My mom is not a teacher.
>
> 저는 가수가 아니에요.
> I'm not a singer.

1 **N이/가 아니다** [i/ga a·ni·da] : **to not be N**

▶ 아니다 is the negative form of 이다 used to negate the noun.

▶ It's used in the form of N이/가 아니다.

▶ However, 이/가 is often omitted in the spoken language.

2 Rules (informal polite form)

If the noun ends with a consonant,	If the noun ends with a vowel,
Noun + 이 아니에요	**Noun** + 가 아니에요
선생님 + 이 아니에요	가수 + 가 아니에요

✓
이/가: Subject Particle
이/가 are actually subject markers, used to indicate the subject of a sentence. You'll learn more about them in Chapter 4.

	Consonant-Ending Nouns	Vowel-Ending Nouns
Formal Polite	N이 아닙니다 [i a·nim·ni·da] 선생님이 아닙니다	N가 아닙니다 [ga a·nim·ni·da] 가수가 아닙니다
Informal Polite	N이 아니에요 [i a·ni·e·yo] 선생님이 아니에요	N가 아니에요 [ga a·ni·e·yo] 가수가 아니에요
Casual	N이 아니야 [i a·ni·ya] 선생님이 아니야	N가 아니야 [ga a·ni·ya] 가수가 아니야

Q: 엄마는 가수예요?   Is your mom a singer?
A: 아니요, 가수가 아니에요.   No, she's not a singer.

Q: 아빠는 선생님이야?   Is your dad a teacher?
A: 아니, 선생님이 아니야.   No, he's not a teacher.

WORDS   아니다 [a·ni·da] to not be

Master Grammar By Practicing!

 02-04P.mp3

A Choose the correct negative form of '이다'.

언니는 선생님 (가 아니에요 / 이 아니에요).	My older sister is not a teacher.

1. 엄마는 의사(가 아닙니다 / 이 아닙니다).   My mom is not a doctor.
2. 저는 대학생(가 아니에요 / 이 아니에요).   I am not a college student.
3. 형은 회사원(가 아니에요 / 이 아니에요).   My older brother is not an office worker.
4. 나는 독일 사람(가 아니야 / 이 아니야).   I am not German.

B Complete the sentences in 3 different styles.

Jenny is not a college student.	제니는 대학생이 아닙니다 / 이 아니에요 / 이 아니야.

1. My mom is not a teacher.   엄마는 선생님_____ / _____ / _____
2. My father is not a doctor.   아버지는 의사_____ / _____ / _____
3. Daniel is not an actor.   다니엘은 배우_____ / _____ / _____
4. Maria is not an office worker.   마리아는 회사원_____ / _____ / _____

C Change the following sentence into a negative sentence.

여동생은 학생이에요.	→	여동생은 학생이 아니에요.

1. 저는 대학생이에요.   →   저는 _____
2. 제니는 한국 사람이야.   →   제니는 _____
3. 남동생은 의사입니다.   →   남동생은 _____
4. 언니는 배우예요.   →   언니는 _____

WORDS   **여동생** [yeo·dong·saeng] younger sister   **남동생** [nam·dong·saeng] younger brother

🎧 02-C.mp3

민호: 안녕하세요! 저는 민호입니다. Hello! I'm Minho.

만나서 반가워요. Nice to meet you.

마리아: 안녕하세요! 저는 마리아예요. Hello! I'm Maria.

민호 씨는 한국 사람이에요? Are you Korean?

민호: 네, 한국 사람이에요. Yes, I'm Korean.

저는 대학생이에요. I am a college student.

마리아 씨는 미국 사람이에요? Are you American?

마리아: 아니요, 미국 사람이 아니에요. No, I'm not American.

독일 사람이에요. I'm German.

NOTE

✏️ Koreans avoid using pronouns like 'You' in English but instead prefer using the other person's name or title. When using honorifics, 씨[ssi] or 님[nim] is added to the end of the name. (e.g. 민호 씨, 마리아 씨)

✏️ In Korean, subject pronouns are often omitted when the context is clear. Therefore, the subject 저는 is sometimes omitted in the conversation.

RECAP CHAPTER 2

❶ N이다: to be N

If the noun ends with a consonant → N + 이에요
If the noun ends with a vowel → N + 예요

	Statement	Question
Formal polite	N입니다	N입니까?
Informal polite	N이에요/예요	N이에요?/예요?
Casual	N이야/야	N이야?/야?

❷ N은/는: Topic Particle

If the noun ends with a consonant → N + 은
If the noun ends with a vowel → N + 는

❸ Yes / No

	Yes	No
Polite	네 or 예	아니요
Casual	응 or 어	아니

❹ N이/가 아니다: to not be N

If the noun ends with a consonant → N + 이 아니에요
If the noun ends with a vowel → N + 가 아니에요

Formal polite	N이/가 아닙니다
Informal polite	N이/가 아니에요
Casual	N이/가 아니야

REVIEW TEST CHAPTER 2

A Choose the appropriate word for (　　).

> 저는 미국 사람(　) 아니에요.
> 저는 한국 사람이에요.

① 가　　　② 는　　　③ 이

B Choose the option with the **incorrectly** paired word.

① teacher - 선생님
② singer - 배우
③ doctor - 의사
④ student - 학생

C Choose the correct sentence.

① 엄마은 선생님이에요.
② 아빠는 의사이 아니에요.
③ 동생은 학생이 아니에요.
④ 형은 대학생예요.

D If I am a girl, how do I refer to my older brother and older sister?

① 오빠, 누나　　　② 오빠, 언니
③ 형, 누나　　　④ 형, 언니

E Choose the appropriate word for (　　).

> 가: 아버지는 의사예요?
> 나: (　　　), 아버지는 선생님이에요.

① 아니　　　②네
③ 응　　　④ 아니요

F Choose the option that is grammatically **incorrect** for the blank space.

> 제니: 마리아 씨는 ＿＿＿예요?
> 마리아: 아니요, 저는 ＿＿＿가 아니에요.

① 배우　　　② 의사
③ 회사원　　　④ 엄마

G Read the following dialogue and choose the correct statement.

> 제니:　안녕하세요! 저는 제니예요.
> 민호:　반갑습니다. 저는 민호입니다.
> 　　　제니 씨는 학생이에요?
> 제니:　아니요, 저는 의사예요.
> 　　　민호 씨는 학생이에요?
> 민호:　네, 저는 학생이에요.
> 　　　저는 한국 사람이에요.
> 　　　제니 씨는 미국 사람이에요?
> 제니:　네, 저는 미국 사람이에요.

① 제니는 학생입니다.
② 제니는 한국 사람이 아닙니다.
③ 민호는 의사입니다.
④ 민호는 미국 사람입니다.

🎧 02-V.mp3

No.	✓	Word	Meaning
1	☐	한국	
2	☐	미국	
3	☐	독일	
4	☐	사람	
5	☐	학생	
6	☐	대학생	
7	☐	선생님	
8	☐	가수	
9	☐	배우	
10	☐	의사	
11	☐	회사원	
12	☐	어머니	
13	☐	엄마	
14	☐	아버지	
15	☐	아빠	
16	☐	언니	
17	☐	오빠	
18	☐	누나	
19	☐	형	
20	☐	동생	
21	☐	남동생	
22	☐	여동생	

It's time to review the new words you've learned in this chapter! Write down the meanings of the words and check the ones you have learned.

Number of words I've learned:

_____ / 22

Korean Etiquette: How to Greet When Meeting Someone New in Korea

Do you have specific words and gestures considered polite when meeting someone new in your country? Let's find out how people typically speak and behave in Korea!

Verbal Greetings

In Korea, when meeting someone for the first time, "안녕하세요? [an·nyeong·ha·se·yo] (Hello!)" is commonly used as a greeting. Especially with new acquaintances, it's customary to always use 존댓말, the formal and polite way of speaking. Using 반말, the casual way of speaking, with someone you've just met is considered quite impolite.

Expressing Pleasure of Meeting

After introducing yourselves, expressing pleasure at getting to know each other is conveyed through phrases like "만나서 반갑습니다 [man·na·seo ban·gap·sseum·ni·da]" or "만나서 반가워요 [man·na·seo ban·ga·wo·yo]" both of which mean "Nice to meet you" in English.

Gestures during Greetings

Unlike some cultures, hugging or kissing on the cheek is not common in Korean greetings. Business situations might involve handshakes, but in everyday scenarios, it's more typical to bow slightly as a sign of respect in Korea. Age plays a role here—if the person is older or in a higher position, a deeper bow may be appropriate.

Casual Greeting Gestures

Have you become close with someone around your age and started using 반말 with each other? If so, you no longer need to bow. Simply say "안녕 [an·nyeong] (Hi!)" while waving your hands when you meet or part ways.

CHAPTER 3
Indicating an Object

 **What you'll learn in this chapter**

In this chapter, you will learn Korean pronouns that refer to objects, such as 'this' and 'that'. By understanding the question word 'what' for inquiring about these objects, you'll develop the ability to ask and answer questions by pointing to objects using new Korean words indicating various objects. Additionally, you will also learn how to express ownership relationships.

UNIT 1 | 이것, 그것, 저것 (this, that, that)

🎧 03-01G.mp3

이것은 핸드폰이에요.　　그것은 책이에요.　　저것은 나무예요.
This is a cellphone.　　That is a book.　　That is a tree.

① 이것 [i·geot]: **this,** 그것 [geu·geot]: **that,** 저것 [jeo·geot]: **that**

▶ 이것 = this thing = this (object close to the speaker)

▶ 그것[1] = that thing = that (object close to the listener)

▶ 저것 = that thing = that (object far from both the speaker and listener)

[1] 그것 is also used to indicate something that is invisible but is known to both people.

그것　　이것

저것　　저것

② Abbreviation of 것 + 은 (topic particle)

	O것 + 은	Abbreviation	Spoken[2]
This	이것은 [i·geo·seun]	이건 [i·geon]	이거 [i·geo]
That	그것은 [geu·geo·seun]	그건 [geu·geon]	그거 [geu·geo]
That	저것은 [jeo·geo·seun]	저건 [jeo·geon]	저거 [jeo·geo]

[2] When speaking, 이거, 그거 and 저거 are the most commonly used form.

이것은 핸드폰이에요. = 이건 핸드폰이에요. = 이거 핸드폰이에요.
This is a cellphone.

그것은 책이에요. = 그건 책이에요. = 그거 책이에요.
That is a book.

저것은 나무예요. = 저건 나무예요. = 저거 나무예요.
That is a tree.

WORDS　　핸드폰 [haen·deu·pon] cellphone　　　　책 [chaek] book　　　　나무 [na·mu] tree

Master Grammar By Practicing!

🎧 03-01P.mp3

A Complete the sentences by looking at the picture.

 Jenny

 Daniel

> 제니: <u>이것</u>은 책이에요. 다니엘 씨, <u>그것</u>은 연필이에요?
> 다니엘: 네, <u>이것</u>은 연필이에요.

1. 제니: 다니엘 씨, _____은 핸드폰이에요?

2. 다니엘: 네, _____은 핸드폰이에요. 제니 씨, _____은 공책이에요?

3. 제니: 네, _____은 공책이에요. _____은 텔레비전이에요?

4. 다니엘: 네, _____은 텔레비전이에요.

B Complete the sentences in three different styles.

> This is a pencil.   <u>이것은</u> / <u>이건</u> (abbreviation) / <u>이거</u> (colloquial) 연필이에요.

1. This is a flower. (close to the speaker)
   _____ / _____ / _____ 꽃이에요.

2. That is a cellphone. (close to the listener)
   _____ / _____ / _____ 핸드폰이에요.

3. That is a tree. (far from both the speaker and the listener)
   _____ / _____ / _____ 나무예요.

4. That is a notebook. (close to the listener)
   _____ / _____ / _____ 공책이에요.

WORDS

연필 [yeon·pil] pencil
텔레비전 [tel·le·bi·jeon] television

공책 [gong·chaek] notebook
꽃 [kkot] flower

🎧 03-02G.mp3

> 이것은 무엇입니까?　　　그거 뭐예요?
> What is this?　　　　　　What is that?

❶ 무엇 [mu·eot] : what

▶ 무엇 is used when asking 'what' questions.

▶ Since it acts like a noun, particles and the verb of '이다' can be attached.

❷ 뭐 [mwo] : Abbreviation of 무엇

▶ 뭐 is the abbreviation of 무엇.[1]

▶ It is more casual, while 무엇 is usually used in formal situations.

¹무엇 → 무어 → 뭐

❸ 무엇/뭐 + 이다(to be) : What is···?

Since 무엇 ends with a consonant,	Since 뭐 ends with a vowel,
무엇 + 이에요?	뭐 + 예요?

	무엇	뭐
Formal Polite	무엇입니까? [mu·eo·sim·ni·kka]	뭐입니까? [mwo·im·ni·kka]
Informal Polite	무엇이에요? [mu·eo·si·e·yo]	뭐예요? [mwo·ye·yo]*
Casual	무엇이야? [mu·eo·si·ya]	뭐야? [mwo·ya]*

*Phrases marked with a red star are mostly used in everyday conversation.

Q: 그거 뭐예요? What is that?　　A: 이거 가방이에요. This is a bag.

Q: 저거 뭐야? What is that?　　A: 저거 남산이야. That is Nam mountain.

WORDS　　가방 [ga·bang] bag　　　　　　　　남산 [nam·san] Nam mountain

Master Grammar By Practicing!

 03-02P.mp3

A Choose the answer that matches the given speech style.

(formal polite)	→	이것은 (무엇입니까? / 무엇이에요?)

1. (informal polite) → 그건 (뭐입니까? / 뭐예요?)
2. (formal polite) → 저것은 (무엇입니까? / 무엇이에요?)
3. (casual) → 이거 (뭐에요? / 뭐야?)
4. (informal polite) → 이건 (뭐야? / 뭐예요?)

B Rewrite the given sentences using abbreviations.

이것은 무엇이에요?	→	이건 뭐예요?

1. 그것은 무엇이에요? → _____
2. 저것은 무엇이야? → _____
3. 이것은 무엇이야? → _____
4. 저것은 무엇이에요? → _____

C Translate the given questions into Korean. Write the question in the same speech style as the answer.

(informal polite)	Q: What is that? →	저거 뭐예요?		A: 저거 꽃이에요.

1. (informal polite) Q: What is this? → _____ A: 그거 카메라예요.
2. (informal polite) Q: What is that? → _____ A: 이거 핸드폰이에요.
3. (casual) Q: What is that? → _____ A: 저거 컴퓨터야.
4. (informal polite) Q: What is that? → _____ A: 저거 모자예요.

WORDS   카메라 [ka·me·ra] camera   컴퓨터 [keom·pyu·teo] computer   모자 [mo·ja] hat

03-03G.mp3

> 이것은 엄마의 가방이에요.
> This is my mom's bag.
>
> 그거 민호의 카메라예요?
> Is that Minho's camera?

1 N의 [ui] : Possessive Particle

▶ 의 indicates possession or ownership.

▶ It's equivalent to the English possessive "'s' or 'of'.

2 Rules

> It is irrelevant whether the noun ends with a vowel or a consonant,
>
> possessor → **N의 N** → possessed noun

✓
As a possessive particle, '의' sounds like '에[e]'. So, you can pronounce it as '에[e]' which is easier.

엄마의 가방 mom's bag
아이의 옷 child's clothes

형의 컴퓨터 brother's computer
선생님의 자동차 teacher's car

이거 엄마의 가방이에요.
저건 선생님의 자동차예요.

This is my mom's bag.
That is my teacher's car.

'의' can be omitted.

→ 이거 엄마 가방이에요.
→ 저거 선생님 자동차예요.

This is my mom's bag.
That is my teacher's car.

WORDS
아이 [a·i] child
친구 [chin·gu] friend

옷 [ot] clothes
자동차 [ja·dong·cha] car

Master Grammar By Practicing!

🎧 03-03P.mp3

A Fill in the blanks appropriately.

| This is my older brother's car. (형) | → | 이것은 <u>형의</u> 자동차예요. |

1. This is my mom's pencil. (엄마) → 이것은 _____ 연필이에요.
2. This is Daniel's camera. (다니엘) → 이것은 _____ 카메라야.
3. This is my grandfather's bag. (할아버지) → 이것은 _____ 가방이에요.
4. This is a child's shoes. (아이) → 이것은 _____ 신발이야.

B Complete the sentences using the given words in an informal polite form.

| | Dad's shoes | → | 이것은 <u>아빠의 신발이에요.</u> |

1. Mom's umbrella → 이것은 _____
2. Younger sister's hat → 이것은 _____
3. Grandmother's notebook → 이것은 _____
4. Child's skirt → 이것은 _____

C Write the answer to the question in negative form omitting '의'.

| Q: 이거 <u>형의 카메라</u>예요? | A: 아니요, <u>형 카메라가 아니에요.</u> |

1. Q: 그거 <u>다니엘의 가방</u>이에요? (polite) A: 아니요, _____
2. Q: 그거 <u>친구의 책</u>이야? (casual) A: 아니, _____
3. Q: 그거 <u>언니의 치마</u>예요? (polite) A: 아니요, _____
4. Q: 그거 <u>할아버지의 자동차</u>야? (casual) A: 아니, _____

WORDS

할아버지 [ha·ra·beo·ji] grandfather 신발 [sin·bal] shoes 우산 [u·san] umbrella
할머니 [hal·meo·ni] grandmother 치마 [chi·ma] skirt

🎧 03-C.mp3

헨리: 수지 씨, 그거 뭐예요? Suzy, what is that?

수지: 이거 한국어 책이에요. This is a Korean book.

그건 헨리 씨 모자예요? Is that your hat?

헨리: 네, 제 모자예요. Yes, it's my hat.

저거 수지 씨 자동차예요? Is that your car?

수지: 아니요, 제 자동차가 아니에요. No, it's not my car.

저거 친구 자동차예요. That's my friend's car.

헨리: 이 그림은 뭐예요? What is this picture?

수지: 이건 남산이에요. This is Nam mountain.

한국의 산이에요. It's a mountain in Korea.

NOTE

✎ 이, 그 and 저 can be placed before nouns to indicate proximity and are used in a manner similar to 'this noun' or 'that noun'. For instance, 이 그림 in the conversation translates to 'this picture'.

WORDS 제 [je] my   한국어 [han·gu·geo] Korean (language)   그림 [geu·rim] picture, painting

RECAP CHAPTER 3

❶ 이것, 그것, 저것: this, that, that

이것: object that is close to the speaker
그것: object that is close to the listener
저것: object that is far from both the speaker and the listener

	+ 은 (topic particle)	Abbreviation	Colloquial
이것	이것은	이건	이거
그것	그것은	그건	그거
저것	저것은	저건	저거

❷ 무엇/뭐: what

	무엇	뭐
Formal polite	무엇입니까?	뭐입니까?
Informal polite	무엇이에요?	뭐예요?
Casual	무엇이야?	뭐야?

❸ 의: Possessive Particle

It is irrelevant whether the noun ends with a vowel or a consonant,

possessor · N의 N · possessed noun

REVIEW TEST CHAPTER 3

A Choose the appropriate word for (   ).

> 제니: 민호 씨, (   ) 텔레비전이에요?
> 민호: 아니요, 저건 컴퓨터예요.

① 그거   ② 저거   ③ 이거

B Choose the option with the **incorrectly** paired word.

① flower - 꽃

② skirt - 치마

③ umbrella - 우산

④ notebook - 연필

C Choose the **incorrect** sentence.

① 이것은 엄마 가방입니다.

② 그거 책의 친구야.

③ 이건 수지 자동차예요.

④ 저거 할머니의 신발이에요.

D Choose the option where the '무엇' is correctly changed to '뭐'.

① 무엇이에요? → 뭐예요?

② 무엇입니까? → 뭐니까?

③ 무엇이야? → 뭐이야?

④ 무엇이야? → 뭐요?

E Choose the correct option.

> That is my grandfather's chair.
> → 그것은 제 _____입니다.

① 할머니의 의자   ② 의자의 할아버지

③ 할아버지의 의자   ④ 의자의 할머니

F Read the following dialogue and choose the **incorrect** statement.

> 태오: 리사 씨, 그거 뭐예요?
> 리사: 이건 아빠 우산이에요. 그건 뭐예요?
> 태오: 이건 형의 가방이에요. 저건 뭐예요?
> 리사: 저건 언니 카메라예요.

① The umbrella of Lisa's dad is close to Lisa.

② The bag of Teo's brother is close to Teo.

③ The camera belongs to Lisa's dad.

④ The camera is far from Teo and Lisa.

G Choose the option that correctly matches all the words in the brackets.

> 수지: 헨리 씨, 그거 뭐에요?
> 헨리: (   ) 핸드폰이에요.
> 수지: 헨리 씨 핸드폰이에요?
> 헨리: (   ), 여동생의 핸드폰이에요.
> 수지: 저건 뭐예요?
> 헨리: (   ) 제 모자예요.

① 저거 - 아니요 - 이건

② 저거 - 네 - 저건

③ 이거 - 네 - 이건

④ 이거 - 아니요 - 저건

🎧 03-V.mp3

No.	✓	Word	Meaning
1	☐	책	
2	☐	공책	
3	☐	연필	
4	☐	그림	
5	☐	우산	
6	☐	가방	
7	☐	옷	
8	☐	신발	
9	☐	모자	
10	☐	치마	
11	☐	꽃	
12	☐	나무	
13	☐	핸드폰	
14	☐	카메라	
15	☐	컴퓨터	
16	☐	텔레비전	
17	☐	자동차	
18	☐	할아버지	
19	☐	할머니	
20	☐	친구	
21	☐	아이	
22	☐	남산	
23	☐	한국어	

It's time to review the new words you've learned in this chapter! Write down the meanings of the words and check the ones you have learned.

Number of words I've learned:

_____ / 23

Exploring Traditional Korean Meals

Korea is a country known for its diverse and delicious cuisine. Surrounded by the sea on three sides and experiencing distinct seasons, Korea has access to a variety of rich and diverse ingredients throughout the year. A typical Korean meal consists of rice, soup, side dishes (반찬 Banchan), and various stews, grilled dishes, and stir-fried dishes.

Rice and Soup (밥 Bap and 국 Guk)
The staple of the Korean diet is rice and soup. Rice can be either white rice or mixed grain rice, and there are various types of soups, including soybean paste soup, bean sprout soup, and seaweed soup.

Side Dishes (반찬 Banchan)
Korean meals are accompanied by a variety of side dishes, with kimchi being the most representative. Other side dishes include various pickled vegetables, dried fish, and seasoned greens. The inclusion of these diverse side dishes enhances the overall richness of a meal.

When dining in Korea, it is common to use both a spoon and chopsticks.

Spoon (숟가락 Sutgarak)
Spoons are mainly used for eating rice and soups. Since rice is usually served in a bowl, people use a spoon to scoop and eat it. Soups, stews, and easily scoopable side dishes are also enjoyed with a spoon.

Chopsticks (젓가락 Jeotgarak)
Chopsticks are commonly used for picking up side dishes, kimchi, meat, and other solid items. In Korea, both metal and wooden chopsticks are commonly used, with metal chopsticks being more prevalent.

CHAPTER 4
Indicating Location

UNIT 1 N이/가 있다 (there is/to have) & N에 ① (at/in)

UNIT 2 여기, 거기, 저기 (here, there) & 어디 (where)

UNIT 3 Positional Words

 **What you'll learn in this chapter**

In this chapter, you will learn how to express the presence or absence of objects in Korean. In addition, you will learn words that indicate location, enabling you to talk about the positions of objects. Throughout this section, you will acquire essential vocabulary related to everyday places. By the end of the chapter, you will be able to express 'what' is located 'where' in Korean.

🎧 04-01G.mp3

방에 책상이 있어요.
There is a desk in the room.

한국 친구가 없어요.
I have no Korean friends.

❶ 있다 [it·tta] : there is/to have

▶ 있다 expresses the location.
방에 책상이 있어요. There is a desk in the room. (A desk is located.)

▶ 있다 also expresses the possession.
저는 책상이 있어요. I have a desk. (I own it.)

❷ N이/가 [i/ga] : Subject Particle

▶ 이/가 is a particle used to indicate the subject of a sentence.[1]

If the noun ends with a consonant,	If the noun ends with a vowel,
Noun + 이 책상 + 이	**Noun + 가** 친구 + 가

❸ Basic Conjugation

	Consonant-Ending Nouns	Vowel-Ending Nouns
Formal Polite	N이 있습니다 [i it·sseum·ni·da]	N가 있습니다 [ga it·sseum·ni·da]
Informal Polite	N이 있어요 [i it·sseo·yo]	N가 있어요 [ga it·sseo·yo]
Casual	N이 있어 [i it·sseo]	N가 있어 [ga it·sseo]

❹ N에 [e] ① : at/in

▶ 에 is a particle used to express the presence of someone or something at a certain place.

방에 책상이 있어요. There is a desk in the room.

✓ 없다[eop·tta]:
The opposite of 있다
방에 책상이 없어요.
There is no desk in the room.
저는 언니가 없어요.
I don't have a sister.

✓ 있다 is typically used in the form of N이/가 있다. However, depending on the context, N은/는 있다 may be used.

[1] See page 70 to learn the difference between 은/는 and 이/가.

✓ 에 always comes after the noun, whether it ends with a consonant or not.
방에 (in the room)
카페에 (at the cafe)

WORDS   방 [bang] room   책상 [chaek·sang] desk   카페 [kka·pe] cafe

Master Grammar By Practicing!

 04-01P.mp3

A Choose the correct option to match the noun.

책상(이 / 가) 있어요.	There is a desk.

1. 의자(이 / 가) 있어요.　　　　　There is a chair.
2. 꽃(이 / 가) 있어요.　　　　　　There are flowers.
3. 컴퓨터(이 / 가) 있어요.　　　　There is a computer.
4. 우산(이 / 가) 있어요.　　　　　There is an umbrella.

B Complete the sentences using the given words according to the given form.

I have an older brother. 오빠 / 있다 (formal polite) → 저는 <u>오빠가 있습니다</u>.	

1. I don't have a car. 자동차 / 없다 (informal polite)　→ 저는 _____
2. I have a younger sister. 여동생 / 있다 (casual)　→ 나는 _____
3. Yuna doesn't have a house. 집 / 없다 (casual)　→ 유나는 _____
4. Jenny has a camera. 카메라 / 있다 (formal polite)　→ 제니는 _____

C Complete the sentences using the given words according to the given form.
('polite' indicates 'informal polite')

<u>There is a chair in the classroom.</u> 교실 / 의자 (polite)　→ <u>교실에 의자가 있어요.</u>	

1. <u>There is a blackboard in the room.</u> 방 / 칠판 (polite)　→ _____
2. <u>There are no</u> books in the coffee shop. 커피숍 / 책 (polite)　→ _____
3. <u>There is no</u> bed in the room. 방 / 침대 (casual)　→ _____
4. <u>There is</u> a computer in the classroom. 교실 / 컴퓨터 (causal)　→ _____

WORDS

의자 [ui·ja] chair	교실 [gyo·sil] classroom	집 [jip] house
칠판 [chil·pan] blackboard	커피숍 [keo·pi·syop] coffee shop	침대 [chim·dae] bed

∩ 04-02G.mp3

> 여기는 학교예요.
> This is a school.

> 가방이 어디에 있어요?
> Where is the bag?

❶ **여기** [yeo·gi]: **here**, **거기** [geo·gi]: **there**, **저기** [jeo·gi]: **there**

▸ 여기 = this place/here (the place close to the speaker)

▸ 거기 = that place/there (the place close to the listener or out of sight)

▸ 저기 = that place/there (the place far from both the speaker and listener)

❷ **어디** [eo·di]: **where**

▸ 어디 is used to ask about the location.

▸ The location particle '에' can be attached.

Q: 책이 어디에 있어요?   Where is the book?
A: 책이 방에 있어요.   The book is in the room.

▸ 어디 + 이다(to be) → 어디이다 (Where is...?)

Formal polite	어디입니까? [eo·di·im·ni·kka]
Informal polite	어디예요? [eo·di·ye·yo]
Casual	어디야? [eo·di·ya]

Q: 여기는 어디예요?   Where is this place?
A: 여기는 공원이에요.   This is a park.

Q: 제니의 집은 어디야?   Where is Jenny's house?
A: 저기야.   It's over there.

✓
You can also use
이곳 (this place),
그곳 (that place),
저곳 (that place)
with 이, 그, 저.
They are usually used in
formal situations.
However, 여기, 거기, and
저기 are more commonly
used.

WORDS   학교 [hak·gyo] school   공원 [gong·won] park

Master Grammar By Practicing!

PRACTICE

🎧 04-02P.mp3

A Look at the picture below and fill in the blanks.

 0. 카페　　 1. 도서관　　 2. 병원　　 3. 식당

Q: 여기는 어디예요? (informal polite)	A: 여기는 <u>카페예요</u>.

1. Q: 여기는 어디입니까? (formal polite)　　A: 여기는 _____
2. Q: 여기는 어디야? (casual)　　A: 여기는 _____
3. Q: 여기는 어디예요? (informal polite)　　A: 여기는 _____

B Choose the correct option to match the previous sentence.

이곳은 학교입니다.	→	(여기 / 저기 / 거기)는 학교예요.

1. 그곳은 거실입니다.　　→　　(여기 / 거기 / 저기)는 거실이에요.
2. 저곳은 도서관입니다.　　→　　(여기 / 거기 / 저기)는 도서관이에요.
3. 이곳은 다니엘의 집입니다.　　→　　(여기 / 거기 / 저기)는 다니엘의 집이에요.

C Fill in the blanks with appropriate questions.

		Q: 여기는 <u>어디예요?</u>	A: 여기는 서점이에요.
		Q: 책은 <u>어디에 있어요?</u>	A: 책은 서점에 있어요.

1. 　은행　Q: 여기는 _____　A: 여기는 은행이에요.
2. 　산　Q: 나무는 _____　A: 나무는 산에 있어요.
3. 　학교　Q: 학생은_____　A: 학생은 학교에 있어요.
4. 　바다　Q: 저기는 _____　A: 저기는 바다예요.

WORDS

도서관 [do·seo·gwan] library	**병원** [byeong·won] hospital	**식당** [sik·dang] restaurant
거실 [geo·sil] living room	**서점** [seo·jeom] bookstore	**은행** [eun·haeng] bank
산 [san] mountain	**바다** [ba·da] sea	

UNIT 3 | Positional Words

🎧 04-03G.mp3

컴퓨터가 책상 위에 있어요.
The computer is on the desk.

가방 안에 책이 있어요.
There's a book in the bag.

❶ Positional Words

▶ Korean positional words describe the position of something.

 상자 앞 [sang·ja ap]
in front of the box

 상자 뒤 [sang·ja dwi]
behind the box

 상자 위 [sang·ja wi]
on top of the box

 상자 아래/밑
[sang·ja a·rae/mit]
under the box

 상자 안 [sang·ja an]
inside the box

 상자 밖 [sang·ja pak]
outside the box

 상자 옆 [sang·ja yeop]
next to the box

 상자 사이 [sang·ja sa·i]
between the box

❷ Rules

The location particle '에' is usually attached.

Noun + ( )[1] + positional word + 에

책상 위에 컴퓨터가 있어요.　　　　　The computer is on the desk.
책상 아래에 신발이 있어요.　　　　　The shoes are under the desk.
의자가 책상 앞에 있어요.　　　　　　The chair is in front of the desk.
피아노가 책상 옆에 있어요.　　　　　The piano is next to the desk.

[1] In between a noun and the positional word, it needs a space.

The position of 'N에' and 'N이/가' can be changed.
컴퓨터가 책상 위에 있어요.
= 책상 위에 컴퓨터가 있어요.

WORDS　　상자 [sang·ja] box　　　피아노 [pi·a·no] piano

Master Grammar By Practicing!

 04-03P.mp3

A Match the pictures with the appropriate positional words.

a 　　b 　　c 　　d 　　e

0. 상자 뒤 (c)　　1. 상자 밖 (　)　　2. 상자 사이 (　)　　3. 상자 위 (　)　　4. 상자 아래 (　)

B Choose the correct option to match the previous sentence.

컴퓨터가 책상 위에 있어요.	→	<u>책상 위에 컴퓨터가</u> 있어요.

1.　집 사이에 자동차가 있어요.　→　_____ 있어요.

2.　책상 뒤에 칠판이 있어요.　→　_____ 있어요.

3.　컵이 창문 앞에 있어요.　→　_____ 있어요.

4.　고양이가 가방 안에 있어요.　→　_____ 있어요.

C Look at the picture on the right and fill in the blanks.

Q: 꽃이 어디에 있어요?
A: 피아노 <u>위에 있어요.</u>

1.　Q: 피아노가 어디에 있어요?　　A: 책상 _____

2.　Q: 우산이 어디에 있어요?　　A: 피아노 _____

3.　Q: 컴퓨터가 어디에 있어요?　　A: 책상 _____

4.　Q: 신발이 어디에 있어요?　　A: 책상 _____

WORDS　　창문 [chang·mun] window　　컵 [keop] cup　　고양이 [go·yang·i] cat

🎧 04-C.mp3

제니: 유나 씨 방에 뭐가 있어요?
        What's in your room?

유나: 제 방에 침대가 있어요.
        There is a bed in my room.

        그리고 창문 앞에 책상이 있어요.
        And there is a desk in front of the window.

제니: 책상 위에 컴퓨터가 있어요? Is there a computer on the desk?

유나: 아니요, 저는 컴퓨터가 없어요. No, I don't have a computer.

        책상 위에 책이 있어요. There are books on the desk.

제니: 유나 씨는 피아노가 있어요? Do you have a piano?

유나: 네, 있어요. Yes, I have.

        피아노는 침대 앞에 있어요. The piano is in front of the bed.

NOTE

✎ 무엇 (abbreviated as 뭐) functions as a subject. In the sentence "뭐가 있어요?" ("What is there?"), the combination of 뭐 (what) and the subject particle 가 (subject particle) forms the subject. You could also ask formally, "무엇이 있습니까?"

WORDS   그리고 [geu·ri·go] and

RECAP CHAPTER 4

❶ N이/가 있다: there is/to have

If the noun ends with a consonant → N + 이
If the noun ends with a vowel → N + 가

	있다 (positive)	없다 (negative)
Formal polite	N이/가 있습니다	N이/가 없습니다
Informal polite	N이/가 있어요	N이/가 없어요
Casual	N이/가 있어	N이/가 없어

❷ N에: at/in

❸ 여기, 거기, 저기: here, there, there

여기: the place close to the speaker
거기: the place close to the listener
저기: the place far from both the the speaker and listener

❹ 어디: where

	어디 + 이다
Formal polite	어디입니까?
Informal polite	어디예요?
Casual	어디야?

❺ Positional Words

앞	in front of	뒤	behind
위	on top of	아래 / 밑	under
안	inside	밖	outside
옆	next to	사이	between

REVIEW TEST CHAPTER 4

A Choose the option that is paired with the correct answers.

> 교실에 칠판(　) 있어요.
> 저는 언니(　) 없어요.

① 이 - 가　　　　② 이 - 이

③ 가 - 이　　　　④ 가 - 가

B Choose the correct sentence.

① 아빠가 집에 있아요.

② 거실에 피아노이 있습니다.

③ 엄마는 자동차가 있어요.

④ 교실에 책상가 있어.

C What is the correct answer for the blank space in the following conversation?

> A: 저기가 _____?
> B: 저기는 남산이에요.

① 어디요?　　　　② 어디예요?

③ 어디에요?　　　④ 어디이니까?

D Choose the option with the **incorrectly** paired word.

① in front of - 옆

② behind - 뒤

③ under - 아래

④ between - 사이

E Look at the picture of the classroom and choose the sentence that corresponds to it.

① 책상 위에 가방이 있어요.

② 나무가 창문 밖에 있어요.

③ 교실에 칠판이 없어요.

④ 책상 아래에 책이 있어요.

F Read the following dialogue and choose the **incorrect** statement.

> 마리아: 여기는 어디예요?
> 다니엘: 여기는 교실이에요.
> 마리아: 다니엘 씨 교실에 칠판이 없어요?
> 다니엘: 네, 칠판이 없어요.
> 마리아: 교실에 뭐가 있어요?
> 다니엘: 컴퓨터가 있어요.
> 마리아: 텔레비전은 있어요?
> 다니엘: 아니요, 없어요.

① 이곳은 다니엘의 교실입니다.

② 교실에 칠판이 없습니다.

③ 교실에 컴퓨터가 없습니다.

④ 교실에 텔레비전이 없습니다.

🎧 04-V.mp3

No.	✓	Word	Meaning
1	☐	집	
2	☐	학교	
3	☐	도서관	
4	☐	서점	
5	☐	병원	
6	☐	은행	
7	☐	식당	
8	☐	카페	
9	☐	커피숍	
10	☐	공원	
11	☐	산	
12	☐	바다	
13	☐	방	
14	☐	거실	
15	☐	교실	
16	☐	침대	
17	☐	책상	
18	☐	의자	
19	☐	피아노	
20	☐	칠판	
21	☐	창문	
22	☐	상자	
23	☐	컵	
24	☐	고양이	
25	☐	그리고	

It's time to review the new words you've learned in this chapter! Write down the meanings of the words and check the ones you have learned.

Number of words I've learned:

_____ / 25

Understanding the Difference Between 은/는 and 이/가

The distinction between the Korean particles '은/는' and '이/가' poses one of the most challenging aspects for Korean learners. Both particles seem to play a role in making a noun the subject of the sentence. However, strictly grammatically, '이/가' serves as the subject case particle, while '은/는' functions as a topic marker. Therefore, in practical usage, distinguishing the subtle differences between the two is genuinely difficult. Nevertheless, let's explore some prominent differences.

은/는: Topic Particle

- **Mark:** the topic of the sentence
- **Meaning:** two hidden meanings
    1) **Topic:** 저는 한국 사람이에요. I'm Korean. (When it comes to me as the topic)
    2) **Contrast:** 책이 책상 위에 있어요. 공책은 책상 위에 없어요.
       The book is on the desk. The notebook is not on the desk. (In contrast to the book)
- **Focus:** on the information following
    엄마는 집에 있어요. My mom is at home.
    (To focus on where she is, rather than who is at home.)
- **은/는** is used when the topic is already known or has been previously mentioned.
    피아노가 있어요. 피아노는 제 방에 있어요. There is a piano. The piano is in my room.

이/가: Subject Particle

- **Mark:** the subject of the sentence
- **Meaning:** no special meaning, just indicating the subject
    책이 책상 위에 있어요. The book is on the desk.
- **Focus:** on the subject
    엄마가 집에 있어요. My mom is at home. (Who is at home is important)
- **이/가** is used when it is mentioned for the first time.
    피아노가 있어요. 피아노는 제 방에 있어요. There is a piano. The piano is in my room.

In summary, while both '은/는' and '이/가' play roles in identifying elements in a sentence, their usage is context-dependent. '은/는' highlights or contrasts information, whereas '이/가' emphasizes the subject. Don't worry too much if you have difficulty distinguishing between these two particles. As you become more familiar with Korean sentences, you will naturally learn to recognize the difference.

CHAPTER 5
Personal Pronouns

What you'll learn in this chapter

In this chapter, you will learn how to refer to people in Korean using pronouns. We will cover 1st person pronouns, including '저' and '나', which we've already learned, as well as 2nd person and 3rd person pronouns in Korean. Since Korean personal pronouns differ significantly from those in English, pay close attention while studying this chapter. After completing this unit, you'll gain more confidence in constructing sentences in Korean.

UNIT 1 | 저/나 (I), 저희/우리 (we)

🎧 05-01G.mp3

> 저는 학생이에요.
> I am a student.

> 저희는 한국 사람이에요.
> We are Korean.

❶ Personal Pronouns

▶ Korean pronouns have formal and informal forms.

저는 학생이에요. (polite)   I am a student.

나는 학생이야. (casual)   I am a student.

▶ Pronouns can be omitted when the context makes it clear who the person is.

(　) 학생이에요?   Are you a student?

아니요, (　) 회사원이에요.   No, I'm an office worker.

❷ First-Person Pronouns

	Polite (Formal)	Casual (Informal)
I	저 [jeo]	나 [na]
We	저희 [jeo·hi]	우리 [u·ri]

❸ First-Person Pronouns with Topic Particle 은/는

	Polite (Formal)	Casual (Informal)
I	저는 [jeo·neun]	나는 [na·neun]
We	저희는 [jeo·hi·neun]	우리는 [u·ri·neun]

저는 의사예요. (polite)   I'm a doctor.

나는 의사야. (casual)   I'm a doctor.

저희는 의사[1]예요. (polite)   We are doctors.

우리는 의사야. (casual)   We are doctors.

[1] Plural forms are not commonly used for nouns in Korean; instead, the singular form typically replaces the plural form.

Master Grammar By Practicing!

🎧 05-01P.mp3

A Choose the correct form of the first-person pronouns.

(singular & polite)	→	(나는 / 저는 / 우리는 / 저희는) 의사입니다.

1. (singular & casual) → (나는 / 저는 / 우리는 / 저희는) 중국 사람이야.
2. (plural & casual) → (나는 / 저는 / 우리는 / 저희는) 배우야.
3. (singular & polite) → (나는 / 저는 / 우리는 / 저희는) 남자입니다.
4. (plural & polite) → (나는 / 저는 / 우리는 / 저희는) 독일 사람이에요.

B Fill in the blanks appropriately using the given style.

I am Jenny. (polite)	→	<u>저는</u> 제니예요.

1. We are students. (polite) → _____ 학생입니다.
2. We are Korean. (casual) → _____ 한국 사람이야.
3. I am a teacher. (casual) → _____ 선생님이야.
4. I am French. (polite) → _____ 프랑스 사람이에요.

C Correct the underlined pronoun when it doesn't match the formality of the sentence.

<u>나는</u> 미국 사람이에요.	(correct / incorrect)	→	<u>저는</u>

1. <u>저희는</u> 회사원이에요. (correct / incorrect) → _____
2. <u>저는</u> 대학생이야. (correct / incorrect) → _____
3. <u>나는</u> 여자예요. (correct / incorrect) → _____
4. <u>저희는</u> 한국 사람이야. (correct / incorrect) → _____

WORDS

중국 [jung·guk] China   남자 [nam·ja] man
프랑스 [peu·rang·seu] France   여자 [yeo·ja] woman

🎧 05-02G.mp3

선생님은 한국 사람이에요?   너는 의사야?
Are you Korean?   Are you a doctor?

❶ Second-Person Pronouns

	Polite (Formal)	Casual (Informal)
You	당신 [dang·sin]	너 [neo]
You (plural)	당신들 [dang·sin·deul]	너희들 [neo·hui·deul]

> ✓ You need to be more careful when using the pronoun 'you' in Korean. It's not used in the same way as in English.

❷ 당신 [dang·sin] : you (polite)

▶ 당신 is a term of address used between husband and wife.

▶ It is commonly used in songs or poems, similar to 그대.

▶ However, be cautious! If used by a stranger, it may sound offensive.
   → This is rarely used in real life!

❸ 너 [neo] : you (casual)

▶ 너 is used only with close friends who are the same age or younger.

❹ Other Polite Ways to Say 'You' in Korean

▶ Omit the pronoun.

   (   ) 학생이에요?   Are you a student?

▶ Address others using their name or title.
   제니는 의사예요? Are you a doctor? (The listener's name is Jenny.)
   토미 씨[1]는 한국어 선생님이에요? Are you a Korean teacher?
   (The listener's name is Tomi.)
   사장님은 프랑스 사람이에요? Are you French? (The listener is the boss.)

[1] 씨 is typically used for someone such as a stranger or a colleague.

WORDS   사장님 [sa·jang·nim] boss, CEO

Master Grammar By Practicing!

 05-02P.mp3

A Fill in the blanks with the correct word, either '너' or '너희들' in a casual form.

| Are you students? (plural) | → | <u>너희들</u>은 학생이야? |

1. Are you American? (singular) → _____는 미국 사람이야?
2. Do you have a piano? (singular) → _____는 피아노가 있어?
3. Do you have a baby? (plural) → _____은 아기가 있어?
4. Are you movie actors? (plural) → _____은 영화배우야?

B Tomi(토미) is a teacher of Jisoo(지수). Choose the correct answer.

| 지수: (당신은 / 선생님은) 한국 사람이에요? |

1. 토미: (당신은 / 너는) 미국 사람이야?
2. 지수: (선생님은 / 너는) 한국어 선생님이에요?
3. 토미: (지수는 / 지수 씨는) 언니가 있어?
4. 지수: (토미는 / 선생님은) 오빠가 있어요?

C Choose the correct option for the questions based on the given answers.

| (너는 / -) 프랑스 사람이에요? | A: 네, 저는 프랑스 사람이에요. |

1. Q: (너는 / 제니 씨는) 선생님이에요?　A: 아니요, 저는 선생님이 아니예요.
2. Q: (- / 너는) 의사예요?　A: 네, 저는 의사예요.
3. Q: (너희들은 / 당신들은) 학생이야?　A: 응, 우리는 학생이야.
4. Q: (너희들은 / -) 영화배우예요?　A: 네, 저희들은 영화배우예요.

WORDS　　아기 [a·gi] baby　　　　영화배우 [yeong·hwa·bae·u] movie actor

🎧 05-03G.mp3

> 이 사람은 누구예요?
> Who is he/she?

> 그 사람은 다니엘이에요.
> He is Daniel.

❶ 그 [geu] : he, 그녀 [geu·nyeo] : she, 그들 [geu·deul] : they

▶ There are third-person pronouns such as 그, 그녀 and 그들 in Korean However, they are never used in spoken languages![1]

❷ How to Say Third-Person Pronouns in Korean

① Repeat the name or the title

제니는 학생이에요. 제니는 미국 사람이에요. Jenny is a student. She is American.

② Point to third-person using 이, 그, 저

이 사람 (this person), 그 사람 (that person), 저 사람 (that person)

저 사람은 의사예요. He is a doctor.

Honorifics (Polite)	Neutral	Casual
이분 [i·bun][2]	이 사람 [i sa·ram]	얘 [yae][3]
그분 [geu·bun]	그 사람 [geu sa·ram]	걔 [gyae]
저분 [jeo·bun]	저 사람 [jeo sa·ram]	쟤 [jyae]

⚠ The honorific level depends on your relationship with the third person.

❸ 누구 [nu·gu] : who

▶ 누구 is a personal pronoun for asking questions.

누구 + 이다(to be) → 누구이다 (Who is...?)

Formal Polite	누구입니까? [nu·gu·im·ni·kka?]
Informal Polite	누구예요? [nu·gu·ye·yo?]
Casual	누구야? [nu·gu·ya?]

이분은 누구입니까? = 이 사람은 누구예요?= 얘는 누구야? = Who is this?

[1] 그, 그녀 and 그들 are used mainly in novels or nonfiction. Originally absent in Korean, pronouns like 'he', 'she' and 'they' were introduced through translated foreign books and are now used in written language.

[2] 분 is the honorific of 사람

[3] 얘 is short for 이 아이 (kid), 걔 is short for 그 아이, 쟤 is short for 저 아이. However, they are not just for kids. They are applicable to anyone who holds a lower status than you.

Master Grammar By Practicing!

 05-03P.mp3

A Change the underlined words to honorific forms.

<u>그 사람</u>은 사장님이에요. →	<u>그분</u>은 사장님이에요.

1. <u>이 사람</u>은 선생님입니다. → _____은 선생님입니다.
2. <u>저 사람</u>은 어머니예요. → _____은 어머니예요.
3. <u>그 사람</u>은 누구예요? → _____은 누구예요?
4. <u>저 사람</u>은 누구입니까? → _____은 누구입니까?

B Daniel is introducing his family to Jenny. Choose the correct third-person pronouns.

This is my dad →	(이분은 / 얘는) 아빠예요.

1. This is my mother. → (저분은 / 이분은) 제 어머니예요.
2. This is my younger brother. → (이분은 / 얘는) 남동생이에요.
3. This is my older brother. → (이분은 / 이 사람은) 형이에요.
4. This is my grandmother. → (얘는 / 이분은) 할머니예요.

C Fill in the blanks with the correct word, choosing between '누구예요?' and '누구야?'.

Who is this? (polite) →	이 사람은 <u>누구예요</u>?

1. Who is she? (casual) → 그 사람은 _____
2. Who is that? (polite) → 저 사람은 _____
3. Who is he? (casual) → 쟤는 _____
4. Who is this? (polite) → 이분은 _____

WORDS   남편 [nam·pyun] husband

UNIT 4 | Possessive Pronouns & 누구의 (whose)

 **GRAMMAR**

🎧 05-04G.mp3

> 제 취미는 수영이에요.
> My hobby is swimming.

> 이거 누구의 책이에요?
> Whose book is this?

① Rules

▶ To change a pronoun into a possessive pronoun, the possessive particle '의' should be added to the pronoun.

	Polite (Formal)	Casual (Informal)
My	저의 [jeo·ui] 제 [je][1] short	나의 [na·ui] 내 [nae][1] short
Our	저희의 [jeo·hi·ui] 저희 [jeo·hi]*의 omitted	우리의 [u·ri·ui] 우리 [u·ri]*의 omitted
Your	당신의 [dang·sin·ui][2]	너의 [neo·ui] 네 [ne][1] short / 니 [ni][3]
His/Her	그분의 [geu·bun·ui] 그분 [geu·bun]*의 omitted	그 사람의 [geu sa·ram·ui] 그 사람 [geu sa·ram]*의 omitted
Whose	누구의 [nu·gu·ui] 누구 [nu·gu]*의 omitted	

제 이름은 민호예요.   My name is Minho.
우리(의) 취미는 수영이야.   Our hobby is swimming.
이거 누구(의) 안경이에요?   Whose glasses are these?

[1] The short forms are used more frequently.

[2] 당신의 is also rarely used in everyday conversations.

[3] 니 (your) is used in everyday life instead of 네 (your) because 네 (your) is pronounced the same as 내 (my). For example, 니 친구 (your friend) is used more often than 네 친구.

우리/저희 is also used to refer to someone very close to me. In this case, it's translated as *my* in English.
우리 엄마: my mom (O)
our mom (X)
저희 아내: my wife (O)
our wife (X)

WORDS

취미 [chwi·mi] hobby	수영 [su·yeong] swimming	이름 [i·reum] name
안경 [an·kyeong] glasses	아내 [a·nae] wife	

Master Grammar By Practicing!

🎧 05-04P.mp3

A Choose the correct possessive pronoun according to the level of politeness.

| 이것은 (내 / 제) 책이에요. | This is my book. |

1. 그건 (내 / 제) 컴퓨터야.　　　　　That is my computer.
2. 얘는 (저희 / 우리) 딸이야.　　　　She is our daughter.
3. (내 / 제) 카메라가 가방 안에 있어요.　My camera is in the bag.
4. 저 사람은 (내 / 제) 아내입니다.　　She is my wife.

B Correct the underlined possessive pronouns, in case it is incorrect.

| My boyfriend is a student. | 네 남자친구는 학생이야. (correct / incorrect → 내) |

1. Is this your bag?　　　　　　　이거 내 가방이야?　　(correct / incorrect → _____)
2. Is your brother at the company?　내 오빠는 회사에 있어?　(correct / incorrect → _____)
3. My job is a doctor.　　　　　　내 직업은 의사야.　　　(correct / incorrect → _____)
4. My name is Suzy.　　　　　　　네 이름은 수지야.　　　(correct / incorrect → _____)

C Choose the correct possessive pronoun from the words and fill in the blanks.

내　　　제　　　네　　　우리　　　저희

| That is my computer. | 그건 내 컴퓨터야. |

1. My parents are teachers.　　→　_____ 부모님은 선생님입니다.
2. Our hobby is shopping.　　　→　_____ 취미는 쇼핑이야.
3. Our son is not at home.　　　→　_____ 아들이 집에 없어요.
4. Is your bed next to the desk?　→　책상 옆에 _____ 침대가 있어?

WORDS

| 딸 [ttal] daughter | 회사 [hoe·sa] company | 직업 [ji·geop] occupation, job |
| 부모님 [bu·mo·nim] parents | 쇼핑 [syo·ping] shopping | 아들 [a·deul] son |

🎧 05-C.mp3

민호: 제인 씨, 이거 뭐예요? Jane, what is this?

제인: 이거 저희 가족 사진이에요. This is a photo of my family.

민호: 이분은 제인 씨의 오빠예요? Is this your older brother?

제인: 아니요, 얘는 제 남동생 대니예요.
No, he is my younger brother Danny.

대니는 대학생이에요. He is a college student.

민호: 제인 씨는 언니가 있어요? Do you have an older sister?

제인: 아니요, 저는 언니가 없어요. No, I don't have an older sister.

민호: 이분은 누구예요? Who is this?

제인: 이분은 저희 할머니예요. She is my grandmother.

민호: 그럼, 이분은 제인 씨 할아버지예요? So, this is your grandfather?

제인: 네, 저희 할아버지예요. He is my grandfather.

WORDS **가족** [ga·jok] family   **사진** [sa·jin] picture, photo   **그럼** [geu·reom] then

RECAP CHAPTER 5

❶ First-person pronouns

	Polite	Casual
I	저	나
My	저의 / 제	나의 / 내
We	저희	우리
Our	저희의	우리의

❷ Second-person pronouns

	Polite	Casual
You	당신	너
Your	당신의	너의 / 네 / 니
You (pl.)	당신들	너희들
Your (pl.)	당신들의	너희의

❸ Third-person pronouns

	Polite	Neutral	Casual
He / She	이 / 그 / 저분	이 / 그 / 저 사람	얘 / 걔 / 쟤
His / Her	이 / 그 / 저분의	이 / 그 / 저 사람의	얘 / 걔 / 쟤
They	이 / 그 / 저분들	이 / 그 / 저 사람들	얘 / 걔 / 쟤들
Their	이 / 그 / 저분들의	이 / 그 / 저 사람들의	얘 / 걔 / 쟤들

❹ 누구: who, 누구의: whose

	누구 + 이다
Formal polite	누구입니까?
Informal polite	누구예요?
Casual	누구야?

REVIEW TEST CHAPTER 5

A Choose the appropriate word for (   ).

> 민호: 이것은 제니 씨의 가방입니까?
>
> 제니: 아니요, 그것은 (   ) 가방이 아닙니다.

① 네   ② 제   ③ 당신의   ④ 내

B Choose the option with an appropriate pronoun that matches the level of politeness.

① 저희는 배우예요.

② 저는 한국어 선생님이야.

③ 나는 중국 사람입니다.

④ 너는 자동차가 있어요?

C Choose the option with an appropriate possessive pronoun that matches the level of politeness.

① 이건 저의 공책이야.

② 저것은 너의 자동차입니까?

③ 이분들은 우리의 부모님이야.

④ 저기가 당신의 집이야?

D Choose the correct arrangement of the words in brackets.

> That is my friend's bag.
> (제, 그것은, 친구의) 가방이에요.

① 제 그것은 친구의 가방이에요.

② 친구의 그것은 제 가방이에요.

③ 그것은 친구의 제 가방이에요.

④ 그것은 제 친구의 가방이에요.

E Suzy and Minho are talking about Maria's grandmother. Choose the **incorrect** part in their conversation.

> 민호: ①수지 씨는 할머니가 있어요?
>
> 수지: 네, ②저는 할머니가 있어요.
>
> 민호: ③그 사람은 독일 사람이에요?
>
> 수지: 아니요, ④할머니는 미국 사람이에요.

G Read the following dialogue and choose the **incorrect** statement.

> 제니: 유나 씨는 동생이 있어요?
>
> 유나: 네, 남동생이 한 명 있어요.
>
>   제 동생은 대학생이에요.
>
> 제니: 동생은 여자친구 있어요?
>
> 유나: 아니요, 걔는 여자친구 없어요.
>
>   그런데 제 오빠는 여자친구가 있어요.
>
> 수지: 오빠의 직업은 뭐예요?
>
> 유나: 오빠는 가수예요.

① 유나는 오빠가 있습니다.

② 유나의 남동생은 여자친구가 있습니다.

③ 유나의 남동생은 대학생입니다.

④ 유나의 오빠는 가수입니다.

🎧 05-V.mp3

No.	✓	Word	Meaning
1	☐	가족	
2	☐	부모님	
3	☐	남편	
4	☐	아내	
5	☐	딸	
6	☐	아들	
7	☐	아기	
8	☐	여자	
9	☐	남자	
10	☐	사장님	
11	☐	프랑스	
12	☐	중국	
13	☐	이름	
14	☐	직업	
15	☐	취미	
16	☐	수영	
17	☐	쇼핑	
18	☐	회사	
19	☐	영화배우	
20	☐	안경	
21	☐	사진	
22	☐	그럼	

It's time to review the new words you've learned in this chapter! Write down the meanings of the words and check the ones you have learned.

Number of words I've learned:

_____ / 22

Must-Visit Spots: Navigating Seoul's Landmarks

Seoul is renowned for offering a diverse mix of culture, historical landmarks, and modern cityscapes. Let me introduce you to some popular attractions for travelers:

경복궁 Gyeongbokgung Palace

Gyeongbokgung Palace is one of South Korea's largest and most significant palaces, serving as the main palace during the Joseon Dynasty. Within the palace grounds, you'll discover beautiful gardens, palace buildings, and the National Folk Museum. Renting and wearing 한복 (Hanbok, traditional Korean clothing) to stroll through Gyeongbokgung can provide a special experience.

남산 Namsan

Namsan is a mountain located in the heart of Seoul, reaching a height of 270 meters, crowned by the Namsan Seoul Tower. Namsan Seoul Tower is one of Seoul's representative landmarks. You can climb to the summit using Namsan's stairway course, and from the observation deck of Seoul Tower, enjoy the panoramic view of Seoul, especially the beautiful night view.

한강 공원 Han River Park

Han River Park is developed along the Han River, providing a space to enjoy the meeting of nature and the urban environment in Seoul. With bicycle paths along the river, you can rent a bike (known as 따릉이 Ddareungi) and enjoy a pleasant ride.

CHAPTER 6
Expressing Actions

What you'll learn in this chapter

Korean verbs come with various conjugations, posing a challenge for learners. In this chapter, you will learn the fundamental verb conjugation. By thoroughly mastering the regular verb changes in the present tense, you will find it easier to grasp the irregular verbs in Chapter 11. This lesson will also provide you with essential expressions for daily life, covering object particle and location particles.

UNIT 1 | V-(스)ㅂ니다

🎧 06-01G.mp3

> 제니가 옵니까?
> Is Jenny coming?

> 언니가 앉습니다.
> My older sister is sitting

❶ V-(스)ㅂ니다 [sseum·ni·da]

▸ ㅂ니다/습니다 is an honorific ending used in formal or public situations.

▸ The question form is V-(스)ㅂ니까 [sseum·ni·kka]?

❷ Rules

Basic form of Korean verbs: verb stem + 다[1]

가다 = 가 (verb stem) + 다   먹다 = 먹 (verb stem) + 다

If the stem ends with a vowel,	If the stem ends with a consonant,
verb stem + ㅂ니다	**verb stem + 습니다**
가다 (to go)	먹다 (to eat)
→ 가 + ㅂ니다 → 갑니다	→ 먹 + 습니다 → 먹습니다

[1] The basic form of the verb (infinitive) is used when looking up the dictionary or conjugating.

	Vowel-Ending Nouns	Consonant-Ending Nouns
Declarative	-ㅂ니다 [-m·ni·da] 가다 → 갑니다	-습니다 [-ssum·ni·da] 먹다 → 먹습니다
Interrogative	-ㅂ니까? [-m·ni·kka] 가다 → 갑니까?	-습니까? [-ssum·ni·kka] 먹다 → 먹습니까?

마리아가 갑니다.   Maria is going.
마리아가 먹습니까?   Is Maria eating?

WORDS

오다 [o·da] to come   앉다 [an·tta] to sit
가다 [ga·da] to go   먹다 [meok·tta] to eat

Master Grammar By Practicing!

🎧 06-01P.mp3

A Choose the correct option for formal polite form.

엄마가 오다.	→	엄마가 (옵니다 / 오습니다).

1. 친구가 먹다. → 친구가 (먹니다 / 먹습니다).
2. 오빠가 일하다. → 오빠가 (일합니다 / 일하습니다).
3. 다니엘이 쉬다. → 다니엘이 (쉽니다 / 쉬습니다).
4. 영화배우가 앉다. → 영화 배우가 (앉니다 / 앉습니다).

B Correct the interrogative form of 'V-(스)ㅂ니다', in case it is incorrect.

여동생이 가습니까? (가다)	(correct / incorrect)	→ 여동생이 <u>갑니까?</u>

1. 제니가 쉽니까? (쉬다)　　　(correct / incorrect)　　→ 제니가 _____
2. 아빠가 자습니까? (자다)　　(correct / incorrect)　　→ 아빠가 _____
3. 형이 공부습니까? (공부하다) (correct / incorrect)　→ 형이 _____
4. 엄마가 앉습니까? (앉다)　　(correct / incorrect)　　→ 엄마가 _____

C Make the sentences using given words.

마리아 / 먹다	→	<u>마리아가 먹습니다.</u>

1. 엄마 / 일하다 → _____
2. 제니 / 자다 → _____
3. 친구 / 앉다 → _____
4. 할머니 / 쉬다 → _____

WORDS

일하다 [il·ha·da] to work (**일**: work)　　　**쉬다** [swi·da] to rest

자다 [ja·da] to sleep　　　**공부하다** [gong·bu·ha·da] to study (**공부**: study)

🎧 06-02G.mp3

책을 읽습니다.
I'm reading a book.

무엇을 마십니까?
What are you drinking?

❶ N을/를 [eul/leul] : Object Particle

▶ 을/를 is the particle that indicates the object of a sentence.

▶ It's attached to a noun.

▶ It is often omitted in everyday conversations.

❷ Rules

If the noun ends with a consonant,	If the noun ends with a vowel,
Noun + 을 책 + 을	Noun + 를 콜라 + 를

저는 책을 읽습니다.   I'm reading a book.

오빠가 콜라를 마십니다.   My brother is drinking cola.

❸ 무엇 (what) + 을/를 (object particle)

Since 무엇 ends with a consonant,	Since 뭐 ends with a vowel,
무엇 + 을	뭐[1] + 를

무엇을 읽습니까? = 뭐를 읽습니까? = 뭘[2] 읽습니까?

→ What are you reading?

[1] 뭐 is the abbreviation of 무엇.

[2] 뭐를 can be shortened to 뭘. It is often used in everyday conversations.

WORDS   읽다 [ik·tta] to read   마시다 [ma·si·da] to drink   콜라 [col·la] cola

Master Grammar By Practicing!

 06-02P.mp3

A Choose the correct object particle.

제니가 콜라(을 / 를) 마십니다.	Jenny drinks cola.

1. 저는 한국어(을 / 를) 공부합니다.   I study Korean.
2. 오빠가 빵(을 / 를) 먹습니다.   My older brother eats bread.
3. 친구가 책(을 / 를) 읽습니다.   My friend reads a book.
4. 마리아가 카메라(을 / 를) 좋아합니다.   Maria likes cameras.

B Fill in the blanks with the correct word, choosing between '을' and '를'.

선생님이 빵을 먹습니다.	My teacher eats bread.

1. 사장님이 무엇____ 좋아합니까?   What does the boss like?
2. 다니엘이 한국어____ 공부합니다.   Daniel studies Korean.
3. 오빠가 뭐____ 마십니까?   What does your brother drink?
4. 남편이 책____ 읽습니다.   My husband reads a book.

C Complete the sentences using the given words, ending in 'V-(스)ㅂ니다'.

선생님 / 콜라 / 마시다	→	선생님이 콜라를 마십니다.

1. 제니 / 책 / 읽다   →   _____
2. 아빠 / 빵 / 먹다   →   _____
3. 동생 / 쇼핑 / 좋아하다   →   _____
4. 아들 / 한국어 / 공부하다   →   _____

WORDS   빵 [bbang] bread   좋아하다 [jo·a·ha·da] to like

UNIT 3 | V-아요/-아 & N에 ② (to)

🎧 06-03G.mp3

다니엘이 서점에 가요.
Daniel is going to the bookstore.

엄마가 한국 드라마를 봐요.
My mom watches Korean dramas.

❶ Rules of Conjugation ①

> If the last vowel of the verb stem is ㅏ or ㅗ → verb stem + 아요
>
> 살다 to live → 살 + 아요 → 살아요
>
> 가다 to go → 가 + 아요[1] → 가요
>
> 오다 to come → 오 + 아요[1] → 와요

앉다 to sit → 앉 + 아요 → 앉아요 / 앉아[2]
자다 to sleep → 자 + 아요 → 자요 / 자
보다 to see → 보 + 아요 → 봐요 / 봐

❷ N에 [e] ②: to

▶ 에 is used to express the direction in which a particular behavior proceeds.

▶ It is irrelevant whether the noun ends with a consonant or not.

   집에 to the house   학교에 to the school

▶ It is mainly used with verbs that express movement.

가다 (to go): 엄마가 은행에 가요.   My mom goes to the bank.
오다 (to come): 친구가 집에 와요?   Is your friend coming home?
앉다 (to sit): 제니가 의자에 앉아요.   Jenny sits on the chair.
타다 (to get in): 아이가 자동차에 타요.   A child gets in the car.

[1] For easy pronunciation, ㅏ and 아 are merged into ㅏ, as well as ㅗ and 아 into 와.

[2] Remove 요 from the conjugated form to create a casual form.

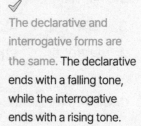

✓ The declarative and interrogative forms are the same. The declarative ends with a falling tone, while the interrogative ends with a rising tone.

✓ To ask 'to where', use 어디에.
어디 + 에 = 어디에
Q: 어디에 가요?
A: 집에 가요.

WORDS

드라마 [deu·ra·ma] drama
살다 [sal·da] to live

보다 [do·da] to see, to watch
타다 [ta·da] to get in, to ride

Master Grammar By Practicing!

🎧 06-03P.mp3

A Match English verbs with their corresponding Korean verbs and their conjugations.

1. to sit	가. 보다	ㄱ. 앉아요	a. 살아
2. to come	나. 앉다	ㄴ. 가요	b. 봐
3. to live	다. 가다	ㄷ. 와요	c. 앉아
4. to go	라. 오다	ㄹ. 살아요	d. 가
5. to see	마. 살다	ㅁ. 봐요	e. 와

B Choose the correct option for informal polite form.

언니가 텔레비전을 (봐요 / 보요).	My older sister watches television.

1. 저는 한국에 (살아요 / 살어요).   I live in Korea.
2. 할아버지가 (자아요 / 자요).   My grandfather sleeps.
3. 마리아가 의자에 (앉아요 / 앉어요).   Maria sits on the chair.
4. 제니가 친구를 (만나아요 / 만나요).   Jenny meets her friend.

C Complete the sentences using the given words in an informal polite form.

다니엘이 어디에 가요? (도서관)	→	다니엘이 <u>도서관에 가요</u>.

1. 선생님이 어디에 와요? (학교)   →   선생님이 _____
2. 오빠가 어디에 가요? (식당)   →   오빠가 _____
3. 아이가 어디에 앉아요? (의자)   →   아이가 _____
4. 할머니가 어디에 타요? (자동차)   →   할머니가 _____

WORDS   만나다 [man·na·da] to meet

🎧 06-04G.mp3

엄마가 책을 읽어요.
My mom is reading a book.

카페에서 친구를 만나요.
I'm meeting my friend at the cafe.

❶ Rules of Conjugation ②

> If the last vowel of the verb stem is neither ㅏ nor ㅗ → **verb stem** + 어요
>
> 먹다 to eat → 먹 + 어요 → 먹어요
>
> 배우다 to learn → 배우 + 어요[1] → 배워요
>
> 마시다 to drink → 마시 + 어요[1] → 마셔요

읽다 to read → 읽 + 어요 → 읽어요 / 읽어[2]

주다 to give → 주 + 어요 → 줘요 / 줘

가르치다 to teach → 가르치 + 어요 → 가르쳐요 / 가르쳐

[1] For easy pronunciation, ㅜ and 어 are merged into 워, as well as ㅣ and 어 into ㅕ.

[2] Remove 요 from the conjugated form to create a casual form.

❷ N에서 [e·seo] : at, in

▶ 에서 is used to express the place at which an action occurs.

▶ It is irrelevant whether the noun ends with a consonant or not.

집에서 at house

학교에서 at the school

아이가 도서관에서 책을 읽어요.
A child reads books at the library.

저는 학교에서 한국어를 배워요.
I learn Korean at school.

친구가 카페에서 콜라를 마셔요.
My friend drinks cola at the cafe.

✓
Use the location particle 에서 to ask where.
어디 + 에서 = 어디에서
Q: 어디에서 책을 읽어요?
A: 집에서 읽어요.

WORDS

배우다 [bae·u·da] to learn
가르치다 [ga·reu·chi·da] to teach

주다 [ju·da] to give

Master Grammar By Practicing!

🎧 06-04P.mp3

A Choose the correct option for informal polite form.

제니가 책을 (읽아요 / 읽어요).	Jenny reads a book.

1. 우리는 콜라를 (마샤요 / 마셔요).　　　　We drink cola.
2. 아빠가 밥을 (먹아요 / 먹어요).　　　　My dad eats rice.
3. 선생님이 한국어를 (가르챠요 / 가르쳐요).　　My teacher teaches Korean.
4. 할머니가 집에서 (쉬어요 / 쉬아요).　　My grandmother takes a rest at home.

B Change the basic verb form to the informal polite and casual forms.

먹다　→　먹어요 / 먹어

1. 주다　→　_____ / _____　　2. 가르치다　→　_____ / _____
3. 읽다　→　_____ / _____　　4. 배우다　→　_____ / _____
5. 마시다　→　_____ / _____

C Complete the sentences using the given words in informal polite form.

제니 / 식당 / 밥 / 먹다　　→　제니가 식당에서 밥을 먹어요.

1. 저 / 학교 / 한국어 / 배우다　→　저는 _____
2. 오빠 / 도서관 / 책 / 읽다　→　오빠가 _____
3. 다니엘 / 교실 / 콜라 / 마시다　→　다니엘이 _____
4. 누나 / 미국 / 한국어 / 가르치다　→　누나가 _____

WORDS　　밥 [bap] rice

🎧 06-05G.mp3

> 저는 매일 운동해요.
> I exercise every day.

> 누가 한국어를 공부해요?
> Who is studying Korean?

❶ 하다[ha·da] Verbs

▶ Many Korean verbs end with 하다.

▶ These verbs consist of a noun plus the ending 하다, meaning 'to do'.

▶ 하다 verbs have unique usage compared to other Korean verbs.

일 work	+ 하다	=	일하다 to work
공부 study	+ 하다	=	공부하다 to study

❷ Rules of Conjugation ③

---

every 하다 → 해요   (하다 → 하 + 여요 → 해요)

일하다 to work → 일해요 / 일해[1]

공부하다 to study → 공부해요/공부해

운동하다 to exercise → 운동해요/ 운동해

요리하다 to cook → 요리해요 / 요리해

[1] Remove 요 from the conjugated form to create a casual form.

❸ 누가[nu·ga]: 'Who' as a Subject

누구 (who) + 가 (subject particle) → 누가 (subject form of 누구)[2]

Q: 누가 식당에 와요?   Who is coming to the restaurant?

A: 제니가 와요.   Jenny is coming.

[2] Use only 누가, not 누구가.

✅
Variations of 누구(who)
누구이다: to be who
누가: who
누구를: whom
누구의: whose

WORDS

운동하다 [un·dong·ha·da] to exercise (운동: exercise)

요리하다 [yo·ri·ha·da] to cook (요리: cook)

Master Grammar By Practicing!

🎧 06-05P.mp3

A Match English verbs with their corresponding Korean verbs and their conjugations.

1.	to do shopping	가. 일하다	ㄱ. 일해요	a. 요리해
2.	to work	나. 쇼핑하다	ㄴ. 요리해요	b. 공부해
3.	to study	다. 공부하다	ㄷ. 운동해요	c. 쇼핑해
4.	to exercise	라. 요리하다	ㄹ. 쇼핑해요	d. 일해
5.	to cook	마. 운동하다	ㅁ. 공부해요	e. 운동해

B Choose the correct form of '누구(who)'.

> Q: 이분은 (누구 / 누가)예요? Who is this?   A: 그분은 제 할머니예요.

1. Q: (누구 / 누가) 식당에 갑니까? Who goes to the restaurant?   A: 여동생이 식당에 갑니다.
1. Q: 이거 (누구의 / 누구를) 연필이에요? Whose pencil is this?   A: 그거 제니의 연필이에요.
1. Q: 다니엘이 (누가 / 누구를) 만나? Who does Daniel meet?   A: 다니엘이 친구를 만나.
1. Q: (누가 / 누구를) 집에서 일해요? Who works at home?   A: 엄마가 집에서 일해요.

C Complete the sentence with the correct form of '누구(who)'.

> Q: 누가 선생님이에요?   A: 토미가 선생님이에요.

1. Q: 이 사람은 _____?   A: 이 사람은 다니엘이에요.
2. Q: _____ 운동해요?   A: 아빠가 운동해요.
3. Q: 이건 _____ 책이에요?   A: 그건 마리아의 책이에요.
4. Q: 엄마가 _____ 사랑해요?   A: 엄마가 아빠를 사랑해요.

WORDS   **사랑하다** [sa·rang·ha·da] to love (**사랑**: love)

🎧 06-C.mp3

헨리: 유나 씨, 어디에 가요? Yuna, where are you going?

유나: 도서관에 가요. I'm going to the library.

헨리: 도서관에서 뭐 해요? What are you doing in the library?

유나: 도서관에서 책 읽어요. I read a book at the library.

　　　헨리 씨는 어디 가요? Where are you going?

헨리: 저는 커피숍 가요. I'm going to a coffee shop.

　　　거기에서 친구를 만나요. I'm meeting a friend there.

유나: 누구 만나요? Who are you meeting?

헨리: 다니엘을 만나요. I'm meeting Daniel.

NOTE

✎ The Korean particles related to location are also used with 여기, 저기, 거기 and 어디. For instance, "거기에 가요? (Are you going there?)". The particle 에 can be omitted in everyday conversations.

✎ The object particle 을/를 is often omitted in everyday conversations, as well as 을 in 무엇을 and 를 in 뭐를 (abbreviation). "뭐 좋아해요?" is more commonly used than "뭐를 좋아해요?" in spoken language.

RECAP CHAPTER 6

❶ Formal polite speech style: V-(스)ㅂ니다

If the verb stem ends with a vowel → verb stem + ㅂ니다
If the verb stem ends with a consonant → N + 습니다

Statement	Question
V-ㅂ니다 / V-습니다	V-ㅂ니까? / V-습니까?
갑니다 / 먹습니다	갑니까? / 먹습니까?

❷ Informal polite speech style: V아/어요, V해요

If the last vowel of the verb stem is ㅏ or ㅗ → verb stem + 아요
If the last vowel of the verb stem is neither ㅏ nor ㅗ → verb stem + 어요
Every verb with 하다 → 하다 changes to 해요

Statement	Question
V-아요 / V-어요 / 해요	V-아요? / V-어요? / 해요?
가요 / 먹어요 / 일해요	가요? / 먹어요? / 일해요?

❸ Casual speech style: V아/어, V해

If the last vowel of the verb stem is ㅏ or ㅗ → verb stem + 아
If the last vowel of the verb stem is neither ㅏ nor ㅗ → verb stem + 어
Every verb with 하다 → 하다 changes to 해

Statement	Question
V-아 / V-어 / 해	V-아? / V-어? / 해?
가 / 먹어 / 일해	가? / 먹어? / 일해?

❹ N을/를, N에, N에서 & 누가

을/를: Object particle
에: Particle indicating the direction where an action proceeds (to)
에서: Particle indicating the location where an action occurs (in, at)
누가: 'Who' used as a subject

REVIEW TEST CHAPTER 6

A Choose the option that matches the verb and conjugation **incorrectly**.

① 오다 - 와요   ② 마시다 - 마셔요

③ 앉다 - 앉어요   ④ 요리하다 - 요리해요

B Choose the option that is paired with the correct answer.

> 저는 빵(   ) 좋아해요.
> 엄마가 한국 드라마(   ) 봐요.

① 을 - 를   ② 을 - 을

③ 를 - 를   ④ 를 - 을

C Choose the correct conjugation of the underlined verb in the formal polite form.

> 저는 회사에서 <u>일하다</u>.
> 제니가 의자에 <u>앉다</u>.

① 합니다 - 앉읍니다

② 일하습니다 - 앉읍니다

③ 일합니다 - 앉습니다

④ 일하습니다 - 앉습니다

D Choose the **incorrect** sentence.

① 언니가 남자친구를 사랑해요.

② 친구가 한국어를 배우아요.

③ 누나가 도서관에서 책을 읽어요.

④ 엄마가 집에서 쉬어요.

E In the following passage, choose the option with the **incorrectly** written particle.

> 다니엘이 ①도서관에 가요. 다니엘은 ②도서관에서 책을 읽어요. 도서관 안에 카페가 있어요. 다니엘은 ③카페에 민호를 만나요. ④카페에서 콜라를 마셔요.

F Choose the sentence where the underlined word is **incorrect**.

① 저 사람은 <u>누구예요</u>?

② 이거 <u>누구의</u> 핸드폰이에요?

③ 제니가 <u>누구를</u> 좋아해요?

④ <u>누구</u> 한국어를 가르쳐요?

G Read the following dialogue and choose the **incorrect** statement.

> 민호: 수지 씨, 어디에 가요?
> 수지: 카페에 가요.
>   거기에서 제니를 만나요.
> 민호: 카페에서 뭐 마셔요?
> 수지: 저는 콜라를 마셔요.
>   민호 씨는 오늘 뭐 해요?
> 민호: 저는 오늘 쇼핑해요.
> 수지: 뭘 사요?
> 민호: 신발을 사요.

① 수지는 카페에 갑니다.

② 수지는 콜라를 마십니다.

③ 민호는 제니를 만납니다.

④ 민호는 신발을 삽니다.

🎧 06-V.mp3

No.	✓	Word	Meaning
1	☐	가다	
2	☐	가르치다	
3	☐	마시다	
4	☐	만나다	
5	☐	먹다	
6	☐	배우다	
7	☐	보다	
8	☐	살다	
9	☐	쉬다	
10	☐	앉다	
11	☐	오다	
12	☐	읽다	
13	☐	자다	
14	☐	주다	
15	☐	타다	
16	☐	공부하다	
17	☐	사랑하다	
18	☐	요리하다	
19	☐	운동하다	
20	☐	일하다	
21	☐	드라마	
22	☐	좋아하다	
23	☐	밥	
24	☐	빵	
25	☐	콜라	

It's time to review the new words you've learned in this chapter! Write down the meanings of the words and check the ones you have learned.

Number of words I've learned:

_____ / 25

Exploring the Diverse World of Korean '방' Culture

In Korea, a '방(room)' isn't just a living space. The concept of 방 has expanded to include spaces created for various cultural activities. Let's explore some of the most renowned '방' experiences in Korea.

노래방 Noraebang

Noraebang is an entertainment venue where individuals or groups can reserve a room to sing songs. It offers a variety of music genres, not limited to Korean pop but also featuring international hits, with real-time updates. The hourly fee system allows customers to enjoy music while ordering drinks and snacks, creating a space for social activities as well.

피씨방 PC Bang

PC Bang is a place where people use personal computers for internet browsing or gaming. These spaces are popular for group gaming sessions, particularly in online games where teams can gather and play together. Similar to noraebangs, PC Bangs usually charge an hourly fee and often provide options to order food and drinks.

찜질방 Jjimjilbang

Jjimjilbang is a unique form of a public bathhouse in Korea, rooted in traditional bathing culture. Jjimjilbangs provide various bathing experiences, including hot baths, cold baths, and herbal baths. Different types of saunas are also available to help relieve fatigue. Many Jjimjilbangs have relaxation rooms with comfortable seating and sleeping spaces with blankets for customers to take a rest. Food and drinks are often available for purchase within jjimjilbang.

CHAPTER 7
Negative Sentences

UNIT 1 안 V / V-지 않아요 (do not)

UNIT 2 못 V / V-지 못해요 (cannot)

UNIT 3 Negation of 하다 Verbs

What you'll learn in this chapter

In this chapter, you'll learn how to negate the verbs covered in the previous chapter. You'll learn the negative forms equivalent to 'do not' and 'cannot' in English. In Korean, there are two different ways to create each negative form. In particular, verbs with 하다 have distinct characteristics from other verbs. By the end of this chapter, you'll also become more familiar with essential Korean verbs for daily life.

UNIT 1 안 V / V-지 않아요 (do not)

🎧 07-01G.mp3

> 저는 커피를 안 마셔요.
> I don't drink coffee.
>
> 저는 커피를 마시지 않아요.
> I don't drink coffee.

❶ Short Negation

안 [an] + verb → do not

먹다 → 안 먹다 to not eat   자다 → 안 자다 to not sleep

저는 고기를 안 먹어요.   I do not eat meat.

아기가 안 자요.   The baby does not sleep.

❷ Long Negation

verb stem + 지 않다 [ji an·ta] → do not

먹다 → 먹지 않다 to not eat   자다 → 자지 않다 to not sleep

Formal Polite	V지 않습니다 [ji an·sseum·ni·da]
Informal Polite	V지 않아요 [ji a·na·yo]
Casual	V지 않아 [ji a·na]

저는 고기를 먹지 않아요.   I do not eat meat.

아기가 자지 않아요.   The baby does not sleep.

Q: 우유를 마셔요?   Do you drink milk?

A: 아니요, 우유를 안 마셔요. or   No, I don't drink milk

아니요, 우유를 마시지 않아요.

✓ The meaning is the same for both negative forms, 안 form and 지 않다 form.

WORDS   커피 [keo·pi] coffee   고기 [go·gi] meat   우유 [u·yu] milk

Master Grammar By Practicing!

🎧 07-01P.mp3

A Match the corresponding words in the short and long negation forms.

1. 앉다	가. 안 살다	a. 쉬지 않다
2. 보다	나. 안 쉬다	b. 앉지 않다
3. 쉬다	다. 안 앉다	c. 살지 않다
4. 배우다	라. 안 배우다	d. 보지 않다
5. 살다	마. 안 보다	e. 배우지 않다

B Change the sentences into short negation form considering the level of politeness.

제니가 책을 읽어요.	→	제니가 책을 <u>안</u> 읽어요.

1. 아이가 밥을 먹어요. → 아이가 밥을 _____
2. 아기가 자요. → 아기가 _____
3. 마리아가 사과를 삽니다. → 마리아가 사과를 _____
4. 다니엘이 한국어를 배워. → 다니엘이 한국어를 _____

C Change the sentences into long negation form considering the level of politeness.

엄마가 커피를 마셔요.	→	엄마가 커피를 <u>마시지 않아요</u>.

1. 선생님이 한국어를 가르쳐요. → 선생님이 한국어를 _____
2. 나는 손을 씻어. → 나는 손을 _____
3. 제니가 지금 드라마를 봐요. → 제니가 지금 드라마를 _____
4. 오빠가 물을 삽니다. → 오빠가 물을 _____

WORDS

사과 [sa·kwa] apple   사다 [sa·da] to buy   씻다 [ssit·tta] to wash
손 [son] hand   지금 [ji·geum] now   물 [mul] water

UNIT 2 | 못 V / V-지 못해요 (cannot)

🎧 07-02G.mp3

> 저는 오늘 일찍 못 자요.
> I can't sleep early today.

> 저는 오늘 일찍 자지 못해요.
> I can't sleep early today.

❶ Short Negation

못 [mot] + verb → cannot

가다 → 못 가다 can't go   마시다 → 못 마시다 can't drink

저는 파티에 못 가요.   I cannot go to the party.

엄마는 술을 못 마셔요.   My mom cannot drink.

❷ Long Negation

verb stem + 지 못하다 [ji mot·ta·da] → cannot

가다 → 가지 못하다 can't eat   마시다 → 마시지 못하다 can't drink

Formal Polite	V지 못합니다 [ji mot·tam·ni·da]
Informal Polite	V지 못해요 [ji mot·tae·yo]
Casual	V지 못해 [ji mot·tae]

저는 파티에 가지 못해요.   I cannot go to the party.

엄마는 술을 마시지 못해요.   My mom cannot drink.

Q: 자전거를 타요?   Do you ride a bike?

A: 아니요, 자전거를 못 타요. or   No, I can't ride a bike.
아니요, 자전거를 타지 못해요.

> ✓ The meaning is the same for both negative forms, 못 form and 지 못하다 form.

WORDS

오늘 [o·neul] today   파티하다 [pa·ti·ha·da] to have a party (파티: party)
술 [sul] drink, alcohol   일찍 [il·jjik] early   자전거 [ja·jeon·geo] bicycle

Master Grammar By Practicing!

🎧 07-02P.mp3

A Match the corresponding words in the short and long negation forms.

1.	열다	가. 못 타다		a. 먹지 못하다
2.	타다	나. 못 열다		b. 만나지 못하다
3.	만나다	다. 못 가르치다		c. 타지 못하다
4.	먹다	라. 못 만나다		d. 열지 못하다
5.	가르치다	마. 못 먹다		e. 가르치지 못하다

B Change the sentences into short negation form considering the level of politeness.

마리아가 한국어를 읽어요.	→	마리아가 한국어를 <u>못 읽어요.</u>

1. 저는 일찍 일어나요. → 저는 일찍 _____
2. 사장님이 집에서 쉬어요. → 사장님이 집에서 _____
3. 친구가 술을 마셔. → 친구가 술을 _____
4. 민호가 자전거를 탑니다. → 민호가 자전거를 _____

C Change the sentences into long negation form considering the level of politeness.

엄마가 한국어를 가르쳐요.	→	엄마가 한국어를 <u>가르치지 못해요.</u>

1. 마리아가 오늘 학교에 가요. → 마리아가 오늘 학교에 _____
2. 나는 한국어를 배워. → 나는 한국어를 _____
3. 동생이 바나나를 먹습니다. → 동생이 바나나를 _____
4. 제니가 파티에 와요. → 제니가 파티에 _____

WORDS

열다 [yeol·da] to open   일어나다 [i·reo·na·da] to get up
자주 [ja·ju] often   바나나 [ba·na·na] banana

07-03G.mp3

저는 운전을 안 해요.
I don't drive.

저는 오늘 운동을 못 해요.
I can't work out today.

❶ Verbs Ending with 하다 [ha·da]

▶ Since 하다 verbs are comprised of Noun + 하다 (to do), they can be divided into Noun을/를 and 하다.

일하다 → 일을 하다 to work
        object

❷ Negation of 하다 Verbs

> Add 안 or 못 between the object and the verb
>
> object + **안 / 못** + 하다

Negation of 일해요

→ 일을 안 해요. I don't work. / 일을 못 해요. I can't work

⚠ 안 일해요 or 못 일해요 → WRONG!

오늘 쇼핑(을)[1] 안 해요. (O)   I don't go shopping today.
오늘 안 쇼핑해요. (X)

저는 노래(를) 못 해요. (O)   I can't sing.
저는 못 노래해요. (X)

Q: 요즘 운동해요?   Do you work out these days?
A: 아니요, 요즘 운동 안 해요.   No, I don't work out these days.

[1] The object particle 을/를 can be omitted. It's especially when there is another object or adverb in front. For example, "저는 한국어를 공부 안 해요." is more natural than "저는 한국어를 공부를 안 해요."

For 'V-지 않다' and 'V-지 못하다', you can either divide or combine the object and the verb '하다'.

일해요 → 일하지 않아요
일을 해요 → 일을 하지 않아요
요리해요 → 요리하지 못해요
요리를 해요 → 요리를 하지 못해요.

WORDS
운전하다 [un·jeon·ha·da] to drive (운전: driving)
노래하다 [no·rae·ha·da] to sing (**노래**: song)   **요즘** [yo·jeum] these days

Master Grammar By Practicing!

🎧 07-03P.mp3

A Change the sentences into short and long negation forms considering the level of politeness.

엄마가 쇼핑해요.	→	엄마가 <u>쇼핑을 안 해요. / 쇼핑하지 않아요.</u>

1. 제니가 오늘 공부해요. → 제니가 오늘 _____ / _____

2. 민호가 운전해. → 민호가 _____ / _____

3. 저는 노래해요. → 저는 _____ / _____

4. 저는 요리합니다. → 저는 _____ / _____

B Change the sentences into short and long negation forms considering the level of politeness.

저는 학교에서 공부해요. →	저는 학교에서 <u>공부를 못 해요. / 공부하지 못해요.</u>

1. 저는 운전해요. → 저는 _____ / _____

2. 다니엘이 오늘 요리해요. → 다니엘이 오늘 _____ / _____

3. 아빠가 청소해. → 아빠가 _____ / _____

4. 선생님이 노래합니다. → 선생님이 _____ / _____

C Correct the sentence, in case it is incorrect.

언니가 안 운전해요.	(correct / incorrect)	→	<u>언니가 운전을 안 해요.</u>

1. 저는 오늘 안 쇼핑해요. (correct / incorrect) → _____

2. 제니가 못 요리해요. (correct / incorrect) → _____

3. 아빠가 노래를 못 해요. (correct / incorrect) → _____

4. 우리는 매일 안 청소해. (correct / incorrect) → _____

> **WORDS**
>
> **샤워하다** [sya·wo·ha·da] to take a shower (**샤워**: shower)
>
> **청소하다** [cheong·so·ha·da] to clean up (**청소**: cleaning)   **매일** [mae·il] every day

🎧 07-C.mp3

요코: 티나 씨는 부산 여행을 가요? Are you going on a trip to Busan?

티나: 아니요, 저는 여행 못 가요. No, I can't go on a trip.

         한국어 시험이 있어요. I have a Korean test.

         그래서 집에서 공부해요. So I study at home.

         요코 씨는 시험 봐요? Are you taking the test?

요코: 아니요, 저는 시험을 보지 않아요. No, I'm not taking the test.

         그래서 여행을 가요. So I'm going on a trip.

티나: 요코 씨가 운전해요? Do you drive?

요코: 아니요, 제 남자친구가 해요. No, my boyfriend does.

         저는 운전을 못 해요. I can't drive.

NOTE

✎ A similar expression to '여행하다' is the phrase '여행(을) 가다 (to go on a trip)'. It's also commonly used.

✎ The phrase 'to take a test' is expressed in Korean using the verb '보다 (to see)', as in '시험을 보다'.

WORDS   부산 [bu·san] Busan   그래서 [geu·rae·seo] so, therefore

RECAP CHAPTER 7

❶ Negation of Korean verbs: '가다(to go)' as an example

	Short form	Long form
do not	안 + verb	verb stem + 지 않다
Formal polite	안 갑니다	가지 않습니다
Informal polite	안 가요	가지 않아요
Casual	안 가	가지 않아
cannot	못 + verb	verb stem + 지 못하다
Formal polite	못 갑니다	가지 못합니다
Informal polite	못 가요	가지 못해요
Casual	못 가	가지 못해

❷ Negation of 하다 verbs: '일하다(to work)' as an example

	Short form	Long form
do not	object + 안 + 하다	verb stem + 지 않다
Formal polite	일을 안 합니다	일하지 않습니다 일(을) 하지 않습니다
Informal polite	일을 안 해요	일하지 않아요 일(을) 하지 않아요
Casual	일을 안 해	일하지 않아 일(을) 하지 않아
cannot	object + 못 + 하다	verb stem + 지 못하다
Formal polite	일을 못 합니다	일하지 못합니다 일(을) 하지 못합니다
Informal polite	일을 못 해요	일하지 못해요 일(을) 하지 못해요
Casual	일을 못 해	일하지 못해 일(을) 하지 못해

REVIEW TEST CHAPTER 7

A Choose the option paired with the correct answer.

> 제니: 다니엘은 고기를 먹어요?
>
> 다니엘: 아니요, 저는 고기를 (   ) 먹어요.
> No, I don't eat meat.
>
> 제니: 그럼 커피를 마셔요?
>
> 다니엘: 아니요, (   ) 않아요.
> No, I don't drink.

① 안 - 마셔　　② 안 - 마시지

③ 못 - 마시지　　④ 못 - 마셔

B Choose the option with the **incorrectly** paired word.

① to take a shower - 샤워하다

② to love - 사랑하다

③ to clean up - 청소하다

④ to cook - 운동하다

C Choose the **incorrect** conjugation for 하다 verbs.

① I don't drive. - 안 운전해요

② I don't work. - 일 안 해요.

③ I don't study. - 공부하지 않아요.

④ I don't sing. - 노래를 안 해요.

D Choose the correct negation of the underlined verb in the formal polite form.

> 저희는 술을 사다. We can't buy alcohol.
>
> 저는 손을 씻다. I don't wash my hands.

① 사지 못합니다 - 씻지 아닙니다

② 사지 못해요 - 씻지 않습니다

③ 사지 못습니다 - 씻지 않아요

④ 사지 못합니다 - 씻지 않습니다

E Choose the correct arrangement of the words in brackets.

> My friend doesn't cook at home.
> (제, 요리를, 여동생은, 안, 집에서) 해요.

① 제 여동생은 요리를 안 집에서 해요.

② 제 여동생은 집에서 안 요리를 해요.

③ 제 여동생은 집에서 요리를 안 해요.

④ 요리를 제 여동생은 안 집에서 해요.

F Read the following dialogue and choose the **incorrect** statement.

> 지수: 유나 씨 언니는 요리를 해요?
>
> 유나: 아니요, 언니는 요리를 못해요.
> 지수 씨 언니는 요리를 해요?
>
> 지수: 네, 요리를 해요.
> 요즘은 요리하지 않아요.
>
> 유나: 언니가 일해요?
>
> 지수: 아니요, 언니는 일을 하지 않아요.
> 언니는 대학생이에요.

① 유나의 언니는 요리를 못합니다.

② 지수의 언니는 요즘 요리하지 않습니다.

③ 지수의 언니는 일을 합니다.

④ 지수의 언니는 대학생입니다.

🎧 07-V.mp3

No.	✓	Word	Meaning
1	☐	사다	
2	☐	씻다	
3	☐	열다	
4	☐	일어나다	
5	☐	노래하다	
6	☐	샤워하다	
7	☐	운전하다	
8	☐	청소하다	
9	☐	파티하다	
10	☐	고기	
11	☐	바나나	
12	☐	사과	
13	☐	물	
14	☐	술	
15	☐	우유	
16	☐	커피	
17	☐	손	
18	☐	자전거	
19	☐	매일	
20	☐	오늘	
21	☐	요즘	
22	☐	일찍	
23	☐	자주	
24	☐	지금	
25	☐	그래서	

It's time to review the new words you've learned in this chapter! Write down the meanings of the words and check the ones you have learned.

Number of words I've learned:

_____ / 25

Exploring Must-Try Korean Dishes ①

Korean cuisine, commonly referred to as '한식 Hansik' is renowned for its distinctive and diverse menus. It encompasses unique and traditional dishes developed in Korea. Hansik utilizes rice, meat, and vegetables, employing various cooking methods and seasonings to create a rich harmony of spicy, savory, and flavorful tastes. Let's explore some representative Korean dishes:

김치 Kimchi

Kimchi is a fermented vegetable dish, typically made with cabbage or various vegetables mixed with red pepper powder. It is a staple in Korean cuisine, served as a side dish during meals and used in various dishes like kimchi stew or kimchi fried rice.

불고기 Bulgogi

Bulgogi is a dish featuring thinly sliced beef marinated in a sweet soy sauce, grilled along with the mix of mushrooms, vegetables, and noodles. Known for its tender texture and sweet flavor, bulgogi is enjoyed by many, even those who may not prefer spicy foods.

삼겹살 Samgyeopsal

Samgyeopsal refers to grilled pork belly, a beloved dish in Korea and often considered a national favorite. It is commonly grilled on a barbecue grill or an open flame and enjoyed by wrapping the meat in lettuce leaves with garlic, peppers, and a dipping sauce.

비빔밥 Bibimbap

Bibimbap is a dish where various vegetables, meat, and an egg are placed on top of rice and mixed with 고추장 gochujang (red pepper paste) and sesame oil. It provides a delicious and nutritious combination of ingredients, with 돌솥 비빔밥 dolsot bibimbap, served in a hot stone bowl, being particularly popular.

CHAPTER 8
Expressing Numbers

What you'll learn in this chapter

In the previous section of this book, we learned how to express numbers in Korean. In this chapter, you will learn how to count things and people, as well as tell time and dates. As you've learned, there are two ways to refer to numbers in Korean, and the numeric form you use depends on what you are expressing. There is much to learn, but since numbers are essential in daily life, try learning them one by one!

UNIT 1 Counting & 몇 (how many)

08-01G.mp3

> 우리 가족은 네 명이에요.   고양이가 두 마리 있어요.
> We are a family of four.   There are two cats.

① Counting Things and People with Counters

▶ Native Korean numbers are used alongside counters (unit word) when counting things or people.

▶ When Korean numbers are used with counters, the form of some numbers changes slightly:

하나 → 한, 둘 → 두, 셋 → 세, 넷 → 네

Example with the counter 개 (개 is used to count things)

1	한 개 [han·gae]	6	여섯 개 [yeo·seot gae]	11	열한 개 [yeol·han gae]	...	...
2	두 개 [du·gae]	7	일곱 개 [il·gop gae]	12	열두 개 [yeol·du gae]	20	스무 개 [seu·mu gae]
3	세 개 [se·gae]	8	여덟 개 [yeo·deol gae]	13	열세 개 [yeol·se gae]	21	스물한 개 [seu·mul·han gae]
4	네 개 [ne·gae]	9	아홉 개 [a·hop gae]	14	열네 개 [yeol·ne gae]	22	스물두 개 [seu·mul·du gae]
5	다섯 개 [da·seot gae]	10	열 개 [yeol gae]	15	열다섯 개 [yeol·da·seot gae]	23	스물세 개 [seu·mul·se gae]

② Counters

People (neutral)	People (honorifics)	Ages	Animals	Things	Bottles	Glasses/ Cups	Books
명 [myeong]	분 [bun]	살 [sal]	마리 [ma·ri]	개 [gae]	병 [byeong]	잔 [jan]	권 [gwon]
한 명 두 명 세 명	한 분 두 분 세 분	한 살 두 살 세 살	한 마리 두 마리 세 마리	한 개 두 개 세 개	한 병 두 병 세 병	한 잔 두 잔 세 잔	한 권 두 권 세 권

몇 [myeot] is a question word used to ask about quantity or number.
→ 'How many' or 'How much' in English

몇 명	몇 분	몇 살	몇 마리	몇 개	몇 병	몇 잔	몇 권

Q: 콜라가 몇 병 있어요?   How many bottles of coke do you have?

A: 두 병 있어요.   I have two bottles.

Q: 몇 살이에요?   How old are you?

A: 저는 스물두 살이에요.   I am twenty-two years old.

Master Grammar By Practicing!

🎧 08-01P.mp3

A Choose the correct option.

two bottles of water	→	물 (두 / 둘) 병

1. a friend   →   친구 (한 / 하나) 명
2. thirteen apples   →   사과 (열 셋 / 열 세) 개
3. four books   →   책 (네 / 넷) 권
4. twenty years old   →   (스물 / 스무) 살

B Fill in the blanks appropriately.

a bottle of cola	→	콜라 <u>한 병</u>

1. four dogs   →   개 _____
2. twelve children   →   아이 _____
3. seven books   →   책 _____
4. two glasses of water   →   물 _____

C Fill in the blanks with the appropriate number and counter.

There are four books on the desk.	→	책상 위에 책이 <u>네 권</u> 있어요.

1. Jenny is 25 years old.   →   제니는 _____ 입니다.
2. There are 11 teachers in the school.   →   학교에 선생님이 _____ 있어요.
3. We buy 5 bottles of Coke.   →   우리는 콜라를 _____ 사요.
4. I drink 3 cups of coffee everyday.   →   나는 매일 커피를 _____ 마셔.

WORDS   개 [gae] dog

UNIT 2 | Telling Time

🎧 08-02G.mp3

지금 몇 시예요?
What time is it now?

지금 열두 시 십 분이에요.
It's ten past twelve now.

❶ Telling Time

▶ 시 [si] is used for hours, with native Korean numbers like 하나, 둘, 셋.

한 시 1 o'clock   다섯 시 5 o'clock

▶ 분 [bun] is used for minutes, with Sino-Korean numbers like 일, 이, 삼.

십 분 10 minutes   이십오 분 25 minutes

o'clock				minutes				
1	한 시 [han si]	7	일곱 시 [il·gop si]	1	일 분 [il bun]	7	칠 분 [chil bun]	13	십삼 분 [sip·sam bun]
2	두 시 [du si]	8	여덟 시 [yeo·deol si]	2	이 분 [i bun]	8	팔 분 [pal bun]	...	...
3	세 시 [se si]	9	아홉 시 [a·hop si]	3	삼 분 [sam bun]	9	구 분 [gu bun]	20	이십 분 [i·sip bun]
4	네 시 [ne si]	10	열 시 [yeol si]	4	사 분 [sa bun]	10	십 분 [sip bun]	30	삼십 분 [sam·sip bun]
5	다섯 시 [da·seot si]	11	열한 시 [yeol·han si]	5	오 분 [o bun]	11	십일 분 [si·bil bun]	40	사십 분 [sa·sip bun]
6	여섯 시 [yeo·seot si]	12	열두 시 [yeol·du si]	6	육 분 [yuk bun]	12	십이 분 [si·bi bun]	50	오십 분 [o·sip bun]

5:05 다섯 시 오 분   **2:10** 두 시 십 분   **6:15** 여섯 시 십오 분

4:53 네 시 오십삼 분   **9:40** 아홉 시 사십 분   **7:25** 일곱 시 이십오 분

2:30 두 시 삼십 분
두 시 반[1]

9:55 아홉 시 오십오 분
열 시 오 분 전[2]

3:50 세 시 오십 분
네 시 십 분 전[2]

[1] 반 [ban] is used to indicate 'half' of a given hour.

[2] 전 [jeon] is used to indicate a specific number of minutes before the next o'clock.

❷ 몇 시 [myeot si] : what time

▶ 몇 시 + 이다(to be) → 몇 시이다 (What time is...?)

Formal Polite	몇 시입니까? [myeot si·im·ni·kka]
Informal Polite	몇 시예요? [myeot si·ye·yo]
Casual	몇 시야? [myeot si·ya]

Q: 지금 몇 시예요?   What time is it now?
A: 한 시 십 분이에요.   It's ten past one.

Master Grammar By Practicing!

🎧 08-02P.mp3

A Match the corresponding times.

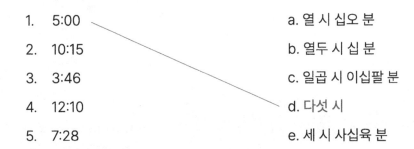

1. 5:00
2. 10:15
3. 3:46
4. 12:10
5. 7:28

a. 열 시 십오 분
b. 열두 시 십 분
c. 일곱 시 이십팔 분
d. 다섯 시
e. 세 시 사십육 분

B Write the given time in a different way using the word '반' or '전'.

| 1:30 한 시 삼십 분 | → | 한 시 반 (half past one) |
| 3:50 세 시 오십 분 | → | 네 시 십 분 전 (10 to 4) |

1. 4:30 네 시 삼십 분   →   _____

2. 2:55 두 시 오십오 분   →   _____

3. 9:30 아홉 시 삼십 분   →   _____

4. 11:50 열한 시 오십 분   →   _____

C Fill in the blanks considering the level of politeness.

| 지금 몇 시예요? | → | (2:30) 두 시 반이에요. |

1. 지금 몇 시입니까?   →   (10:00) _____

2. 지금 _____?   →   (5:10) 다섯 시 십 분이야.

3. 지금 _____?   →   (1:20) 한 시 이십 분이에요.

4. 지금 몇 시예요?   →   (3:15) _____

🎧 08-03G.mp3

언제 친구를 만나요?
When are you meeting your friend?

오후 두 시에 만나요.
I'm meeting him at 2 o'clock in the afternoon.

① Times of the Day

오전 [o·jeon] AM / before noon[1]		오후 [o·hu] PM / afternoon
아침 [a·chim] **morning / breakfast**[2] approx. 6:00-9:00	점심 [jeom·sim] **noon time / lunch** approx. 12:00-13:00	저녁 [jeo·nyeok] **evening / dinner** approx. 18:00-21:00
낮 [nat] **day, day time** approx. 12:00-15:00	밤 [bam] **night, night time** approx. 21:00-0:00	새벽 [sae·byeok] **dawn** approx. 0:00-6:00

`7:00` 아침 일곱 시
오전 일곱 시

`11:00` 오전 열한 시

`14:00` 낮 두 시
오후 두 시

`19:00` 저녁 일곱 시

`22:00` 밤 열 시

`3:00` 새벽 세 시

[1] 오전 means 'before noon (=정오 [jeong·o])' and 오후 means 'after noon'.

[2] 아침, 점심 and 저녁 also refer to 'meal' and 'meal time'.

아침에 공부해요.
I study in the morning.

아침을 먹어요.
I eat breakfast.

✓

In Korean, the 12-hour system is used in most situations. Therefore, you typically use one of these words before stating the time. However, breakpoints in time may vary from person to person.

② N에 [e] ③: at/on

▶ 에 is used to refer to a time when an action takes place.

저녁 일곱 시에 영화를 봐요. I watch a movie at 7 p.m.

▶ It is irrelevant whether the noun ends with a consonant or not.

아침에 in the morning   오후에 in the afternoon

③ 언제 [eon·je]: when

▶ **언제** is used to ask questions about time.

Q: 언제[3] 학교에 가요?   When do you go to school?

A: 오전 7시에 가요.   I go to school at 7 AM.

[3] not 언제에 (X)

④ 몇 시에 [myeot si·e]: what time

▶ This can be used instead of 언제, when asking about a specific time.

Q: 몇 시에 학교에 가요?   What time do you go to school?

Master Grammar By Practicing!

🎧 08-03P.mp3

A Choose the correct option.

| 7:00 A.M. | → | (오전 / 오후) 일곱 시 |

1. 6:00 P.M. → (아침 / 저녁) 여섯 시
2. 10:00 P.M. → (낮 / 밤) 열 시
3. 9:00 A.M. → (아침 / 점심) 아홉 시
4. 4:00 P.M. → (오전 / 오후) 네 시

B Fill in the blanks with the appropriate terms with '에'.

| I usually study in the morning. | → | 저는 주로 아침에 공부해요. |

1. I'm meeting a friend in the afternoon. → 저는 _____ 친구를 만나요.
2. I exercise every morning. → 저는 매일 _____ 운동해요.
3. I usually watch movies at night. → 나는 주로 _____ 영화를 봐.
4. I often sleep during the day. → 저는 자주 _____ 자요.

C On the right is the daily schedule of Minji(민지). Fill in the blanks appropriately.

Q: 민지는 몇 시에 일어나요?
A: 아침 일곱 시에 일어나요.

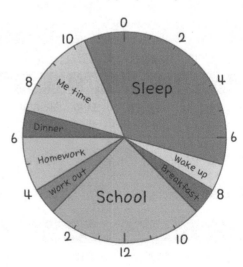

1. Q: 민지는 몇 시에 아침을 먹어요?
   A: _____ 에 아침을 먹어요.

2. Q: 민지는 몇 시에 학교에 가요.
   A: _____ 에 학교에 가요.

3. Q: 민지는 몇 시에 운동해요?
   A: _____ 에 운동을 해요.

4. Q: 민지는 몇 시에 저녁을 먹어요?
   A: _____ 에 저녁을 먹어요.

🎧 08-04G.mp3

> **오늘은 며칠이에요?**
> What's today's date?

> **오늘은 사월 십일이에요.**
> Today is the 11th of April.

① 년 [nyeon] : year

몇 년? [myeot nyeon]	What year?

1992년	→	천구백구십이년	2023년	→	이천이십삼년

✓ For years, months and dates, Sino-Korean numbers are used.

② 월 [wol] : month

몇 월? [myeot wol]	What month?

1월	2월	3월	4월	5월	6월	7월	8월	9월	10월	11월	12월
일월	이월	삼월	사월	오월	유월*	칠월	팔월	구월	시월*	십일월	십이월

* For easier pronunciation, 육월 becomes 유월, and 십월 becomes 시월.

③ 일 [il] : day

며칠? [myeo·chil] (not 몇 일) What day?

1일	2일	3일	4일	5일	6일	7일	8일	9일	10일
일일	이일	삼일	사일	오일	육일	칠일	팔일	구일	십일
11일	12일	13일	14일	15일	16일	17일	18일	19일	20일
십일일	십이일	십삼일	십사일	십오일	십육일	십칠일	십팔일	십구일	이십일
21일	22일	23일	24일	25일	26일	27일	28일	29일	30일	31일
이십일일	이십이일	이십삼일	이십사일	이십오일	이십육일	이십칠일	이십팔일	이십구일	삼십일	삼십일일

④ 요일 [yo·il] : day of the week

무슨 요일? [mu·seon yo·il]	What day of the week?

Monday	Tuesday	Wednesday	Thursday	Friday	Saturday	Sunday
월요일	화요일	수요일	목요일	금요일	토요일	일요일
[wo·ryo·il]	[hwa·yo·il]	[su·yo·il]	[mo·gyo·il]	[geu·myo·il]	[to·yo·il]	[i·ryo·il]

Master Grammar By Practicing!

🎧 08-04P.mp3

A Write the years using Sino-Korean numbers.

1998년	→	천구백구십팔년

1. 2013년 → _____
2. 1780년 → _____
3. 1995년 → _____
4. 2006년 → _____

B Write the dates using Sino-Korean numbers.

오늘은 며칠이에요? (Aug 25, 8월 25일)	→	팔월 이십오일이에요.

1. 오늘은 며칠이에요? (Jun 19, 6월 19일) → _____이에요.
2. 오늘은 며칠이에요? (Dec 26, 12월 26일) → _____이에요.
3. 오늘은 며칠이에요? (Oct 6, 10월 6일) → _____이에요.
4. 오늘은 며칠이에요? (May 31, 5월 31일) → _____이에요.

C Look at the calendar and answer the questions.

내일은 무슨 요일이에요?
→ 일요일이에요.

1. 오늘은 무슨 요일이에요?
   → _____

2. 오늘은 며칠이에요?
   → _____

3. 팔월 십육일은 무슨 요일이에요?
   → _____

4. 며칠에 한국에 가요?
   → _____

8월

월	화	수	목	금	토	일
	1	2	3	4	5	6
7	8	9	10	11	12	13
14	15	16	17	18	19	20
21	22	23	24	25	26	27
28	29	30	31			

Today

Going to Korea

🎧 08-05G.mp3

> 오전 9시부터 오후 5시까지 일해요.
> I work from 9 am to 5 pm.
>
> 집에서 학교까지 걸어가요.
> I walk from home to school.

❶ N부터 N까지 [-bu·teo -kka·ji] : from N to/until N

▶ -부터 -까지 is used to express the temporal range over which an action occurs.

월요일부터 금요일까지	from Monday to Friday
일곱 시부터 여덟 시까지	from seven to eight

❷ N에서 N까지 [-e·seo -kka·ji] : from N to N

▶ -에서 -까지 is used to express the locational range.

여기에서 학교까지	from here to school
서울에서 부산까지	from Seoul to Busan

✅ 에서 and 부터 are sometimes used interchangeably.

🔥 **Useful Korean Phrase**

O 시간이 걸리다: It takes O hours

- 시간 serves as a counting unit when specifying the duration of time.
- This phrase is commonly used to express the time required for an action.

집에서 학교까지 한 시간[1] 걸려요.
It takes an hour from home to school.

[1]이 can be omitted:
  O 시간이 걸려요
  = O 시간 걸려요

Master Grammar By Practicing!

🎧 08-05P.mp3

A Fill in the blanks using '부터' and '까지' appropriately.

I work from 9 AM until 5 PM.	→ 오전 9시<u>부터</u> 오후 5시<u>까지</u> 일해요.

1. Jenny learns Korean starting from tomorrow.   → 제니가 내일_____ 한국어를 배워요.
2. The exam is from Monday to Wednesday.   → 월요일_____ 수요일_____ 시험이에요.
3. We don't go to school until December 3rd.   → 우리는 12월 3일_____ 학교에 안 가.
4. From what time does the store open?   → 가게가 몇 시_____ 열어요?

B Choose the appropriate option.

2월 5일(에서 / 부터) 2월 10일까지 시험이에요.

1. 서울(에서 / 부터) 부산까지 4시간 걸려요.
2. 저는 월요일(에서 / 부터) 금요일까지 일해요.
3. 오후 한 시(에서 / 부터) 두 시까지 점심을 먹어요.
4. 집(에서 / 부터) 학교까지 자전거를 타요.

✓ Switching '에서' and '부터' is not actually an incorrect expression, but try choosing the most appropriate word.

C Complete the conversation by filling in the blanks.

Q: 며칠<u>부터</u> 며칠<u>까지</u> 시험이에요? (from Tuesday to Friday)
A: <u>화요일부터</u> <u>금요일까지</u> 시험이에요.

1. Q: 몇 시____ 몇 시____ 영화를 봐? (from 2 to 4 o'clock)   A: _____ 영화를 봐.
2. Q: 몇 시____ 운동해요? (until 8 o'clock)   A: _____ 운동해요.
3. Q: 언제____ 한국어 공부해요? (from January 1st)   A: _____ 한국어 공부해요.
4. Q: 무슨 요일____ 영국에 있어요? (until Sunday)   A: _____ 영국에 있어요.

WORDS

| **내일** [nae·il] tomorrow | **시험** [si·heom] exam, test | **가게** [ga·ge] store, shop |
| **영화** [yeong·hwa] movie | **영국** [yeong·guk] England | |

🎧 08-C.mp3

제니: 헨리 씨, 지금 몇 시예요? Henry, what time is it now?

헨리: 두 시예요. It's two o'clock.

제니: 몇 시에 한국어 수업이 있어요? What time is the Korean class?

헨리: 세 시부터 다섯 시까지예요. It's from three to five.

저니 씨는 수업에 와요? Are you coming to class?

제니: 저는 오늘 수업에 못 가요. I can't go to class today.

카페에서 네 시부터 아르바이트해요. I work part-time at a cafe from 4 o'clock.

그런데 한국어 시험이 언제예요? By the way, when is the Korean test?

헨리: 10월 5일이에요. It's October 5th.

제니: 저는 내일부터 공부해요. I will start studying tomorrow.

NOTE

🖋 아르바이트 is a term borrowed from the German word 'Arbeit', meaning 'work' or 'job'. In Korean, it refers to part-time or temporary work, often taken on by students.

WORDS

수업 [su·eop] class, lesson

그런데 [geu·reon·de] however, by the way

아르바이트 [a·reu·ba·i·teu] part time job

RECAP CHAPTER 8

❶ Counting things and people: with native Korean numbers

People (neutral)	People (honorifics)	Ages	Animals	Things	Bottles	Glasses	Books
명	분	살	마리	개	병	잔	권
한 명 두 명 세 명	한 분 두 분 세 분	한 살 두 살 세 살	한 마리 두 마리 세 마리	한 개 두 개 세 개	한 병 두 병 세 병	한 잔 두 잔 세 잔	한 권 두 권 세 권
몇 명	몇 분	몇 살	몇 마리	몇 개	몇 병	몇 잔	몇 권

❷ Telling time and dates

O'clock	Minutes	Year	Month	Date	Days of the week
시	분	년	월	일	요일
한 시 두 시 세 시	일 분 이 분 삼 분	일년 이년 삼년	일월 이월 삼월	일일 이일 삼일	월요일, 화요일, 수요일, 목요일 금요일, 토요일, 일요일
몇 시	몇 분	몇년	몇월	며칠	무슨 요일

❸ Times of the day

오전 AM		오후 PM	
아침 morning / breakfast	점심 noon time / lunch		저녁 evening / dinner
낮 day	밤 night		새벽 dawn

❹ N에, 언제, N부터/에서 N까지

에: Particle indicating the time or date when an action occurs (at/on)

언제: Question word asking about time (when)

부터: Particle indicating the temporal starting point (from)

에서: Particle indicating the locational starting point (from)

까지: Particle indicating both the temporal and locational endpoints (until)

REVIEW TEST CHAPTER 8

A Choose the **incorrect** counter that corresponds to each type of word.

① 명 for people

② 권 for books

③ 병 for cups

④ 마리 for animals

B Choose the option that correctly reads the given date.

> August 23, 2023

① 이천이십삼년 칠월 이십삼일

② 이천이십삼년 팔월 이십삼일

③ 이천이십사년 칠월 이십삼일

④ 이천이십삼년 팔월 십삼일

C Choose the option that **incorrectly** reads the time.

① 7:20 - 일곱 시 이십 분

② 12:30 - 열두 시 반

③ 10:50 - 열 시 십 분 전

④ 2:35 - 두 시 삼십오 분

D Choose the option paired with the correct answer.

> A: 지금 (　　)예요?
> B: 지금 두 시 반이에요.
> A: 오늘 (　　)이에요?
> B: 오늘은 수요일이에요.

① 몇 시 - 며칠　　② 몇 월 - 무슨 요일

③ 몇 월 - 며칠　　④ 몇 시 - 무슨 요일

E In the following passage, choose the option written **incorrectly**.

> 지수가 가게에서 ①콜라 두 병을 사요. 서점에서 ②책 한 분을 사요. 오후 ③두 시에 친구를 만나요. 지수는 ④커피 한 잔을 마셔요.

F Choose the sentence where the underlined word is correct.

① 오늘은 <u>무슨 월</u>이에요?

② <u>언제에서</u> 영국에 가요?

③ <u>몇 요일</u>에 집에서 쉬어요?

④ <u>언제부터</u> 한국어를 배워요?

G Read the following dialogue and choose the **incorrect** statement.

> 수지: 민호 씨는 언제 서울 여행가요?
> 민호: 칠월 오일부터 여행해요.
> 수지: 서울까지 몇 시간 걸려요?
> 민호: 여기에서 서울까지 네 시간 걸려요.
> 　　　저는 자동차를 타요.
> 수지: 며칠까지 서울에 있어요?
> 민호: 십일까지 있어요.

① 민호는 서울에서 여행합니다.

② 서울까지 네 시간이 걸립니다.

③ 민호는 칠월 오일까지 서울에 있습니다.

④ 민호는 자동차를 탑니다.

🎧 08-V.mp3

No.	✓	Word	Meaning
1	☐	걸리다	
2	☐	개	
3	☐	가게	
4	☐	영국	
5	☐	영화	
6	☐	수업	
7	☐	시험	
8	☐	시간	
9	☐	아르바이트	
10	☐	서울	
11	☐	부산	
12	☐	내일	
13	☐	그런데	

It's time to review the new words you've learned in this chapter! Write down the meanings of the words and check the ones you have learned.

Number of words I've learned:

_____ / 13

South Korea's Currency: Stories Behind Bills and Coins

The currency presently in use in South Korea includes bills of 50,000 won, 10,000 won, 5,000 won, and 1,000 won denominations, along with coins of 500 won, 100 won, and 10 won.

The 50,000 won bill features Shin Saimdang, a prominent figure during the mid-Joseon period, Shin Saimdang is admired not only as an ideal mother who raised her son Yi I to be an outstanding scholar but also as an accomplished artist in painting and calligraphy.

The 10,000 won bill features King Sejong, who created Hangeul for Korean people struggling with learning Chinese characters and being unable to read and write.

The 5,000 won bill features Yi I. A scholar and politician during the mid-Joseon period, Yi I pursued various social reforms for the welfare of the people.

The 1,000 won bill features Toegye Yi Hwang, a Confucian scholar and philosopher during the Joseon era.

The 500 won coin features a crane, symbolizing South Korea's second economic leap and its emergence onto the international stage.

The 100 won coin depicts Admiral Yi Sun-sin, a brilliant military strategist of the Joseon-era who led the Korean navy to victory in numerous battles against foreign invasions.

The 50 won coin, engraved with rice stalks, commemorates World Food Day on October 16 as part of the UN-initiated FAO Coin Program in 1968. South Korea joined, symbolizing rice as a main staple.

The 10 won coin features the Dabo Pagoda. Situated in Bulguksa Temple in Gyeongju, the Dabo Pagoda is a stone tower from the Silla period, designated as National Treasure No. 20.

CHAPTER 9
Basic Particles

What you'll learn in this chapter

You already know that particles play a crucial role in shaping the meaning of words and sentences in Korean. Thus far, you've covered the subject particle, object particle, and particles indicating time and place. In this chapter, you will delve into a few more essential Korean particles. Mastering these particles will enable you to use new verbs and express yourself more diversely.

N와/과, N(이)랑, N하고 (and/with)

09-01G.mp3

저는 라면하고 김치를 좋아해요.
I like ramyeon and kimchi.

저는 부모님이랑 같이 살아요.
I live together with my parents.

1 N와/과 [wa/kwa], N(이)랑 [i·rang], N하고 [ha·go] : and

▶ These particles are used to connect nouns for listing objects.

2 Rules

If the noun ends with a vowel,	If the noun ends with a consonant,
Noun + 와, 랑, 하고[1]	**Noun + 과, 이랑, 하고**[1]
영어와 한국어 English and Korean	책상과 의자 desk and chair
강아지랑 고양이 dog and cat	연필이랑 공책 pencil and notebook
콜라하고 우유 cola and milk	신발하고 옷 shoes and clothes

저는 영어와 한국어를 배워요.   I'm learning English and Korean.

나는 강아지랑 고양이를 좋아해.   I like dogs and cats.

저는 콜라하고 우유를 안 마셔요.   I don't drink cola and milk.

3 N와/과 [wa/kwa], N(이)랑 [i·rang], N하고 [ha·go] : with

▶ They can also indicate who the subject is doing something with.

▶ You can use words like 같이 [ga·chi] or 함께 [ham·kke] with them to talk about doing things together.

친구와 함께 = 친구랑 같이 = 친구하고 같이 = with friend

친구랑 (같이) 공부해요.   I'm studying (together) with my friend.

가족과 (함께) 여행을 합니다.   I travel (together) with my family.

나는 내 남동생하고 (같이) 살아. I live (together) with my younger brother.

[1] 하고 is irrelevant whether the noun ends with a vowel or a consonant.

✓ While (이)랑 and 하고 are commonly used in everyday conversations, 와/과 is typically used for formal situations such as writing, presentations or official speeches. (이)랑 is the most casual option.

✓ 함께 is usually used with 와/과, and 같이 is usually used with (이)랑 and 하고.

라면 [ra·myeon] ramyeon   **김치** [kim·chi] kimchi   **영어** [yeong·eo] English

강아지 [gang·a·ji] puppy   **여행하다** [yeo·haeng·ha·da] to travel (**여행**: trip)

Master Grammar By Practicing!

🎧 09-01P.mp3

A Choose the correct option.

커피(와 / 과) 빵	커피(랑 / 이랑) 빵
1. 학생(와 / 과) 선생님	학생(랑 / 이랑) 선생님
2. 나무(와 / 과) 꽃	나무(랑 / 이랑) 꽃
3. 사과(와 / 과) 바나나	사과(랑 / 이랑) 바나나
4. 산(와 / 과) 바다	산(랑 / 이랑) 바다

B Rewrite the two words using 'and' in the three forms, as shown in the example below.

주스, 콜라	→	주스와 콜라 / 주스랑 콜라 / 주스하고 콜라

1. 독일, 프랑스 → _____ / _____ / _____
2. 요리, 운동 → _____ / _____ / _____
3. 가방, 핸드폰 → _____ / _____ / _____
4. 책, 연필 → _____ / _____ / _____

C Fill in the blank using the expression 'together with' with the given particle.

(이)랑	→	저는 제니랑 같이 학교에 가요.

1. 와/과 → 카페에서 친구_____ 주스를 마셔요.
2. 하고 → 언니_____ 백화점에서 쇼핑을 해요.
3. 와/과 → 부엌에서 동생_____ 요리해요.
4. (이)랑 → 저는 형_____ 살아요.

WORDS **주스** [ju·sseu] juice   **부엌** [bu·eok] kitchen   **백화점** [baek·hwa·jeom] department store

UNIT 2 | N(이)나, N 아니면 N (or)

🎧 09-02G.mp3

> 토요일이나 일요일에 운동해요.
> I exercise on Saturday or Sunday.
>
> 아침에 커피 아니면 주스를 마셔요.
> I drink coffee or juice in the morning.

❶ N(이)나 [i·na] : or

▶ N(이)나 is used when one of the listed objects can be chosen.

❷ Rules

If the noun ends with a consonant,	If the noun ends with a vowel,
Noun + 이나	**Noun + 나**
연필이나 펜 pencil or pen	커피나 주스 coffee or Juice

가방에 연필이나 펜이 있어?   Do you have a pencil or pen in your bag?

저는 아침에 커피나 주스를 마셔요.   I drink coffee or juice in the morning.

❸ N 아니면 N [a·ni·myeon] : or

아니	+	면	=	if not
stem of 아니다 (to not be)		if		

> ✓ When there are more than three options, (이)나 is listed between each noun.
>
> 저는 아침에 물이나 커피나 주스를 마셔요.
> I drink water, coffee, or juice in the morning.

▶ 아니면 literally translates to 'if not', but in Korean, it's commonly used as a way to express 'or'.

▶ It's positioned between two nouns or two sentences.

▶ 아니면, similar to (이)나, is often used in everyday conversations.

저는 아침에 커피 아니면 주스를 마셔요.
I drink coffee or juice in the morning.

아침에 커피를 마셔요? 아니면 주스를 마셔요?
Do you drink coffee in the morning? Or do you drink juice?

Master Grammar By Practicing!

🎧 09-02P.mp3

A Choose the correct option.

아침에 밥(이나 / 나) 빵을 먹어요.	I eat rice or bread in the morning.

1. 집에 엄마(이나 / 나) 아빠가 있어요?   Is your mom or dad at home?

2. 저는 매일 한국어(이나 / 나) 영어를 공부해요.   I study Korean or English every day.

3. 주말에 다니엘(이나 / 나) 민호를 서점에서 만나요. I meet Daniel or Minho on the weekend.

4. 오늘 밤에 영화(이나 / 나) 드라마를 봐요?   Are you watching a movie or a drama tonight?

B Fill in the blanks appropriately.

7월이나 8월에 한국에 가요.

1. 할머니_____ 할아버지가 병원에 가요?

2. 저는 보통 저녁에 우유_____ 물을 마셔요.

3. 침대 위에 그림_____ 사진이 있어요?

4. 학교_____ 도서관_____ 집에서 공부해요.

C Rewrite the sentences using the expression '아니면'.

저는 주로 사과나 바나나를 먹어요.	→	저는 주로 사과 아니면 바나나를 먹어요.

1. 저는 보통 콜라나 주스를 마셔요.   → _____

2. 월요일이나 화요일에 병원에 가요.   → _____

3. 오빠가 버스나 자전거를 타요.   → _____

4. 내일이나 주말에 여자친구를 만나요.   → _____

WORDS

주말 [ju·mal] weekend   **보통** [bo·tong] normally

주로 [ju·ro] usually   **버스** [beo·seu] bus

🎧 09-03G.mp3

저는 사과를 좋아해요. 바나나도 좋아해요.　언니는 집에서만 공부해요.
I like apples. I also like bananas.　　 My sister studies only at home.

❶ N도 [do]: also/too

▶ 도 is attached to a noun and is used to express that the mentioned noun shares the same action or characteristic as the previous one.

① When 도 is added to topic(은/는), subject(이/가), or object particles(을/를), they are omitted, and only 도 remains.

나는 BTS를 좋아해. 세븐틴도 좋아해.(O)[1]
I like BTS. I also like Seventeen.

[1] 세븐틴을도 좋아해.(X)

② When 도 is added to other particles, they are not omitted but 도 comes after the particles.

저는 오늘 회사에서 일해요. 집에서도 일해요.(O)[2]
I work at the company today. I work from home too.

[2] 집도 일해요.(X)

❷ N만 [man]: only/just

▶ 만 is used to indicate exclusivity or limitation.

① When 만 is added to topic(은/는), subject(이/가), or object particles(을/를), they are omitted, and only 만 remains, or used together like 만은, 만이 or 만을.

제니만 학생이에요.(O) = 제니만이 학생이에요.(O)[3] Only Jenny is a student.

한국어만 공부해요.(O) = 한국어만을 공부해요. (O)[4] I study only Korean.

[3] 제니이만 학생이에요.(X)

[4] 한국어을만 공부해요.(X)

② When 만 is added to other particles, they are not omitted but 만 comes after the particles, similar to 도.

우리 가족은 집에서만 밥 먹어요.(O)[5] My family have a meal only at home.

오늘은 오후 네 시까지만 일해요.(O)[6] I work only until 4 pm today.

[5] 우리 가족은 집만에서 밥 먹어요.(X)

[6] 오늘은 오후 네 시만까지 일해요.(X)

Master Grammar By Practicing!

🎧 09-03P.mp3

A Choose the correct option.

> 저는 제니의 파티에 가요. 다니엘(은도 / 도) 파티에 가요.

1. 저는 민호를 알아요. 마리아(도 / 를도) 알아요.

2. 아빠가 저를 기다려요. 엄마(가도 / 도) 저를 기다려요.

3. 제니는 주로 아침에 운동해요. 저녁(에도 / 도) 운동해요.

4. 저는 보통 방에서 밥을 먹어요. 그리고 가끔 부엌(도 / 에서도) 밥을 먹어요.

B Choose the correct options.

> 제니는 빵(만 / 을만) 먹어요. 밥은 먹지 않아요.

1. 저는 도서관(만 / 에서만) 공부해요. 집에서 공부하지 않아요.

2. 토미 선생님은 한국어(만 / 을만) 가르쳐요. 영어를 안 가르쳐요.

3. 저는 아침(만에 / 에만) 커피를 마셔요. 저녁에 마시지 않아요.

4. 학교에서 지수(만 / 가만) 한국 사람이에요.

C Correct the underlined words.

> 그 은행은 저녁 다섯 시<u>만까지</u> 열어요. → <u>다섯 시까지만</u>

1. 저는 라면을 좋아해요. <u>떡볶이를도</u> 아주 좋아해요. → _____

2. <u>오빠는만</u> 프랑스에 가요. 저는 안 가요. → _____

3. 제니는 <u>미국만</u> 운전해요. 한국에서 안 해요. → _____

4. 형은 주로 아침에 공부해요. <u>밤도</u> 공부해요. → _____

WORDS

알다 [al·da] to know
떡볶이 [tteok·bok·kki] tteokbokki

기다리다 [gi·da·ri·da] to wait
아주 [a·ju] very

UNIT 4 N에게/한테 (to)

🎧 09-04G.mp3

> 선생님에게 편지를 보내요.
> I'm sending a letter to my teacher.
>
> 친구한테서 전화가 와요.
> I'm getting a call from my friend.

❶ N에게 [e·ge], N한테 [han·te] : **to**

▶ 에게 or 한테 are used to indicate the recipient of an action.

▶ They are used only for people or animals.

▶ 에게 is more formal, while 한테 is more colloquial in casual settings.

저는 주말에 할머니에게 가요.   I go to my grandmother on the weekends.
친구한테 전화해요.   I'm calling my friend.

Verbs used with 에게/한테

주다 [ju·da]	to give	보내다 [bo·nae·da]	to send
가다 [ga·da]	to go	오다 [o·da]	to come
선물하다 [seon·mul·ha·da]	to present	팔다 [pal·da]	to sell
전화하다 [jeon·hwa·ha·da]	to call	말하다 [mal·ha·da]	to talk
가르치다 [ga·leu·chi·da]	to teach		

> ✓
> 에 is used for other than people or animals such as plants, things or places.
>
> 나무에 물을 줘요.
> I'm watering the tree.
>
> 회사에 전화해요.
> I'm calling the company.
>
> 학교에 편지를 써요.
> I'm writing a letter to school.

❷ N에게(서) [e·ge·seo], N한테(서) [han·te·seo] : **from**

▶ 에게서 or 한테서 are used when receiving or learning something from someone.

▶ 서 can be omitted.

에게서 → 에게   한테서 → 한테
토미에게서 한국어를 배워요. = 토미에게 한국어를 배워요.
토미한테서 한국어를 배워요. = 토미한테 한국어를 배워요.
I'm learning Korean from Tomi.

WORDS

편지 [pyeon·ji] letter   보내다 [bo·nae·da] to send   선물하다 [seon·mul·ha·da] to present (선물 gift)
팔다 [pal·da] to sell   말하다 [mal·ha·da] to talk (말 talk)   전화하다 [jeon·hwa·ha·da] to call (전화 call)

Master Grammar By Practicing!

🎧 09-04P.mp3

A Choose the correct option.

저는 친구(에 / 에게) 편지를 보내요.	I send a letter to my friend.

1. 저는 내일 할머니(에/ 에게) 가요.   I'm going to my grandmother tomorrow.
2. 오빠가 회사(에 / 에게) 이메일을 보내요.   My brother sends an email to the company.
3. 엄마가 꽃(에 / 에게) 물을 줘요.   My mom waters the flowers.
4. 엄마가 선생님(에 / 에게) 전화해요.   My mom calls my teacher.

B Correct the underlined particle.

저는 누나에게서 선물을 줘요.	→	저는 누나에게 생일 선물을 줘요.

1. 제니가 학교에게 전화해요.   →   제니가 학교_____ 전화해요.
2. 토미가 제니에 한국어를 가르쳐요.   →   토미가 제니_____ 한국어를 가르쳐요.
3. 친구에 선물을 받아요.   →   친구_____ 선물을 받아요.
4. 오빠가 아빠에게서 말해요.   →   오빠가 아빠_____ 말해요.

C Choose the correct option and make sentences with given words.

I give Jenny a gift. (제니, 에/에게, 선물, 주다)	→	제니에게 선물을 줘요.

1. I talk to my mom. (엄마, 한테서/한테, 말하다)   → _____
2. I send my friend email. (친구, 에게/에, 이메일, 보내다)   → _____
3. I learn Korean from Tomi. (토미, 에게/에, 한국어, 배우다) → _____
4. I go to my younger sister. (여동생, 에게/에, 가다)   → _____

WORDS 이메일 [i·me·il] email   받다 [bat·tta] to receive

UNIT 5 N(으)로 (to/with)

🎧 09-05G.mp3

> 고양이가 나무 위로 가요.
> The cat is going up the tree.
>
> 저는 친구랑 자전거로 여행해요.
> I travel by bike with my friend.

❶ N(으)로 [eu·ro] ①: to, toward

▶ (으)로 is used to indicate the direction or destination toward which an action is directed.

| 저는 지금 집으로 가요. | I'm going home now. |
| 저는 왼쪽으로 가요. | I'm going left. |

❷ N(으)로 [eu·ro] ②: with, by

▶ (으)로 is also used to indicate the means or method by which an action is carried out.

| 친구가 자동차로 서울에 가요. | My friend is going to Seoul by car. |
| 마리아가 한국어로 노래해요. | Maria sings in Korean. |

❸ Rules

If the noun ends with a vowel or ㄹ,	If the noun ends with a consonant,
Noun + 로	**Noun + 으로**
학교로, 자동차로	집으로, 밥으로

우리는 바다로 여행가요.　　　　We're going on a trip to the sea.

비빔밥은 밥으로 만들어요.　　　Bibimbap is made with rice.

집에서 학교까지 자전거로 20분 걸려요.
It takes 20 minutes by bike from home to school.

WORDS

왼쪽 [oen·jjok] left side　　　　비빔밥 [bi·bim·bap] bibimbap
만들다 [man·deul·da] to make

Master Grammar By Practicing!

🎧 09-05P.mp3

A Choose the correct option.

개가 책상 아래 (로 / 으로) 가요.	The dog goes under the desk.

1. 선생님이 학교(로 / 으로) 와요.   The teacher comes to the school.
2. 고양이가 오른쪽(로 / 으로) 가요.   The cat goes to the right.
3. 저는 선물을 다니엘의 집(로 / 으로) 보내요.   I send a gift to Daniel's house.
4. 아이하고 엄마가 저 가게(로 / 으로) 가요.   The child and mom go to that store.

B Fill in the blank with 로 or 으로 appropriately.

한국에서 독일까지 비행기로 13시간이 걸려요.

1. 저는 자주 핸드폰_____ 영화를 봐요.
2. 할머니가 저에게 컴퓨터_____ 이메일을 보내요.
3. 저는 한국어를 책_____ 공부해요.
4. 제니가 기차_____ 한국을 여행해요.

C Choose the sentence (A or B) in which the underlined part is used in the same way.

A ◀ 제니가 도서관으로 가요.   저는 미국에 비행기로 가요. B

저는 학교에 자전거로 가요.	(A / B)

1. 할머니랑 할아버지가 우리 집으로 와요.   (A / B)
2. 제니가 친구에게 한국어로 말해요.   (A / B)
3. 집에서 남산까지 자동차로 가요.   (A / B)
4. 아이가 책상 위로 가요.   (A / B)

WORDS   **오른쪽** [o·reun·jjok] right side   **기차** [gi·cha] train   **비행기** [bi·haeng·gi] airplane

🎧 09-C.mp3

민호: 수지 씨는 제니 생일 파티에 가요? Are you going to Jenny's birthday party?

수지: 네, 저는 가요. 마리아하고 같이 가요. Yes, I'm going. I go together with Maria.

민호 씨도 가요? Are you going, too?

민호: 아니요, 저는 못 가요. No, I can't go.

제니한테 선물만 보내요. I'm only sending a gift to Jenny.

수지 씨는 뭐 선물해요? What are you giving to her as a present?

수지: 옷이나 신발을 사요. I buy clothes or shoes.

민호: 제니는 뭘 좋아해요? What does Jenny like?

수지: 제니는 신발 좋아해요. She likes shoes.

그리고 가방도요. And bags, too.

NOTE

✎ In conversations, it's common to respond with just a single word instead of a complete sentence. For instance, when asked, "What do you drink?" one might reply, "Cola." In Korean, it's common to add '요' for politeness. Therefore, to the question "뭐 마셔요?", the polite answer would be "콜라요." not "콜라".

WORDS 생일 [saeng·il] birthday

RECAP CHAPTER 9

❶ N와/과, N(이)랑, N하고: and/with

1. Particle used to connect nouns, indicating the meaning of 'and'
2. Particle indicating whom the subject is doing something with

If the noun ends with a vowel → N + 와, 랑, 하고
If the noun ends with a consonant → N + 과, 이랑, 하고

❷ N(이)나, N 아니면 N: or

(이)나   Particle used to connect nouns, indicating the meaning of 'or'
아니면   Expression equivalent to '(이)나'

If the noun ends with a vowel → N + 나
If the noun ends with a consonant → N + 이나

❸ N도: also, N만: only

도   Particle indicating the meaning of 'also' or 'too'
만   Particle indicating the meaning of 'only' or 'just'

❹ N에게, N한테: to

Particles indicating the recipient of an action, meaning 'to'

❺ N(으)로: to/with

1. Particle indicating the direction or destination, meaning 'to' or 'toward'
2. Particle indicating the means or method, meaning 'with' or 'by'

If the noun ends with a vowel → N + 로
If the noun ends with a consonant → N + 으로

REVIEW TEST CHAPTER 9

A Choose the option paired with the correct answers.

> 저는 고양이 한 마리( ) 개 한 마리가 있어요.
> 책상 위에 연필( ) 공책이 있어요.

① 와 - 와   ② 와 - 과

③ 과 - 와   ④ 과 - 과

B Choose the **incorrect** sentence.

① 제니가 엄마와 아빠에게 선물을 줘요.

② 저기에 신발하고 우산이 있어요.

③ 저는 비빔밥랑 김치를 먹어요.

④ 형과 누나는 대학생이에요.

C Choose the correct sentence.

① 엄마가 영화를 봐요. 아빠도 영화를 봐요.

② 도서관에서 공부해요. 집도 공부해요.

③ 저는 비빔밥을 좋아해요. 라면을도 좋아해요.

④ 토요일에 많이 자요. 일요일도에 많이 자요.

D In the following passage, choose the option that is written **incorrectly**.

> 마리아는 요즘 한국 ①드라마만을 봐요. 집에서 ②마리아만 봐요. 마리아는 드라마를 ③핸드폰만으로 봐요. 마리아는 밤 ④열 한시까지만 드라마를 봐요.

E Choose the sentence where the underlined word is **incorrect**.

① 오늘 다니엘<u>한테</u> 전화해요.

② 아빠가 <u>회사에</u> 이메일을 보내요.

③ 저는 매일 <u>꽃에게</u> 물을 줘요.

④ 선생님이 <u>학생에게</u> 한국어를 가르쳐요.

F Choose the option that is grammatically correct for the blank space.

> 제니가 ____로 가요.
> ____으로 드라마를 봐요.

① 바다 - 컴퓨터   ② 은행 - 컴퓨터

③ 은행 - 핸드폰   ④ 바다 - 핸드폰

G Read the following dialogue and choose the **incorrect** statement.

> 유코: 헨리 씨 보통 몇 시에 일어나요?
> 헨리: 저는 여섯 시나 일곱 시에 일어나요.
>   유코 씨도 일찍 일어나요?
> 유코: 네, 저는 일요일에만 일찍 안 일어나요.
>   헨리 씨는 아침에 뭐 마셔요?
> 헨리: 저는 커피나 우유를 마셔요.
>   빵도 먹어요. 유코 씨도 커피 마셔요?
> 유코: 아니요, 저는 커피를 안 마셔요.
>   저는 아침으로 밥을 먹어요.

① 헨리는 여섯 시 아니면 일곱 시에 일어납니다.

② 유코는 일요일에만 일찍 일어납니다.

③ 헨리는 아침으로 빵을 먹습니다.

④ 유코는 커피를 마시지 않습니다.

🎧 09-V.mp3

No.	✓	Word	Meaning	No.	✓	Word	Meaning
1	☐	기다리다		17	☐	선물	
2	☐	만들다		18	☐	영어	
3	☐	받다		19	☐	이메일	
4	☐	보내다		20	☐	편지	
5	☐	알다		21	☐	주스	
6	☐	팔다		22	☐	김치	
7	☐	말하다		23	☐	떡볶이	
8	☐	여행하다		24	☐	라면	
9	☐	전화하다		25	☐	비빔밥	
10	☐	강아지		26	☐	오른쪽	
11	☐	기차		27	☐	왼쪽	
12	☐	버스		28	☐	보통	
13	☐	비행기		29	☐	아주	
14	☐	백화점		30	☐	주로	
15	☐	부엌		31	☐	주말	
16	☐	생일					

Number of words
I've learned:

_____ / 31

Korean Traditional Holidays: Seollal and Chuseok

설날 Seollal (Korean New Year's Day)

Korean New Year's Day, known as '설날 (Seollal)', is one of Korea's major traditional holidays, signifying the beginning of the lunar new year on the 1st day of the lunar calendar. Seollal spans several days and is designated as a legal holiday.

During Seollal, many people travel from different places to their hometowns to reunite with family members. Younger family members, such as grandchildren, visit relatives, bow to them as a sign of respect, and receive New Year's money and gifts, a custom known as '세배 (Saebae)'.

A representative food for Seollal is '떡국 (Tteokguk)', a soup with sliced rice cakes. Eating Tteokguk is believed to add one more year to a person's age. The tradition of beginning the new year with white-colored food, such as 떡 (tteok), symbolizes a clean and pure mindset for the new year. Additionally, the shape of the sliced rice cakes resembles ancient coins, symbolizing a wish for increased wealth when consuming tteokguk.

추석 Chuseok (Korean Harvest Festival)

Chuseok falls on the 15th day of the lunar calendar, typically in September according to the solar calendar. It is considered a representative autumn holiday in Korea, expressing gratitude for the year's harvest and providing an opportunity to visit hometowns and family.

On Chuseok, families come together to make traditional rice cakes called '송편 (Songpyeon)' and prepare abundant dishes, holding a memorial service for ancestors called '차례 (Charye)' to express gratitude. Sharing a meal together strengthens family bonds.

CHAPTER 10
Describing Traits

 What you'll learn in this chapter

In this chapter, you will learn about Korean adjectives. In Chapter 6, you covered Korean verbs and their conjugation. Korean adjectives share the same form as verbs and adhere to the same rules for conjugation. Once you grasp Korean adjectives, you'll delve into constructing comparative and superlative sentences in Korean. Naturally, this chapter will also introduce you to the essential Korean adjective words.

🎧 10-01G.mp3

방이 작아요.   오늘 날씨가 어때요?
The room is small.   How is the weather today?

❶ Korean Adjectives

▶ Their forms look like verbs ending with 다 such as '작다', '비싸다', '길다'.
▶ They conjugate in the same way as verbs.

❷ Rules of Conjugation in Informal Polite Form

> If the last vowel of the stem is ㅏ or ㅗ → stem + 아요
>
> 작다 → 작아요   비싸다 → 비싸 + 아요 → 비싸요
>
> If the last vowel of the stem is neither ㅏ nor ㅗ → stem + 어요
>
> 길다 → 길어요   흐리다 → 흐리 + 어요 → 흐려요
>
> For all of the adjectives ending with 하다 → stem + 해요
>
> 따뜻하다 → 따뜻해요

신발이 작아요.   The shoes are small.
아이폰이 아주 비싸요.   IPhone is very expensive.
오늘 날씨가 따뜻해요.   The weather is warm today.

❸ 어떻다 [eo·tteo·ta] : to be how

▶ 어떻다 is an adjective that is used to ask about the condition or state of something.

Formal polite	Informal polite	Casual
어떻습니까?	어때요?	어때?
[eo·tteot·sseum·ni·kka]	[eo·ttae·yo]	[eo·ttae]

Q: 오늘 날씨가 어때요?   How is the weather today?

어떻게
It's the adverbial form of '어떻다', meaning 'how' or 'in what way' in English.
Q: 어떻게 지내요?
How are you doing?
A: 잘 지내요.
I'm fine.

WORDS
작다 [jak·tta] to be small   날씨 [nal·ssi] weather   비싸다 [bi·ssa·da] to be expensive
길다 [gil·da] to be long   흐리다 [heu·ri·da] to be cloudy   따뜻하다 [tta·tteut·ta·da] to be warm

Master Grammar By Practicing!

🎧 10-01P.mp3

A Choose the correct option.

집이 (작아요 / 작어요)	The house is small.

1. 커피가 (따뜻하요 / 따뜻해요).   The coffee is warm.
2. 컴퓨터가 조금 (비싸아요 / 비싸요).   The computer is a little expensive.
3. 아이스크림이 (맛있아요 / 맛있어요).   The ice cream is delicious.
4. 연필이 (길어요 / 길아요).   The pencil is long.

B Change the ending form of the adjectives in informal polite form.

날씨가 시원하다.	→	날씨가 시원해요.

1. 라면이랑 김치가 맛있다.   →   라면이랑 김치가 _____
2. 가방이 정말 싸다.   →   가방이 정말 _____
3. 오빠의 자동차가 작다.   →   오빠의 자동차가 _____
4. 오늘 날씨가 좋다.   →   오늘 날씨가 _____

C Choose the appropriate form of '어떻다' considering the level of the politeness.

어떻습니까?	어때요?	어때?

Q: 커피가 어때? (casual)	A: 커피가 따뜻해.

1. Q: 오늘 한국 날씨는 _____ ? (informal polite)   A: 날씨가 좋아요.
2. Q: 콜라가 _____ ? (informal polite)   A: 콜라가 시원해요.
3. Q: 비빔밥이 _____ ? (formal polite)   A: 비빔밥이 아주 맛있습니다.
4. Q: 그 옷은 _____ ? (casual)   A: 이 옷은 조금 작아.

WORDS

조금 [jo·geum] a little   아이스크림 [a·i·seu·keu·rim] ice cream   맛있다 [ma·sit·tta] to be delicious
싸다 [ssa·da] to be cheap   정말 [jeol·mal] really   좋다 [jo·ta] to be good

UNIT 2 | N보다 (than), 더 (more), 덜 (less)  GRAMMAR

🎧 10-02G.mp3

> 미국이 독일보다 더 멀어요.
> The United States is further away than Germany.

> 영화보다 드라마가 덜 재미있어요.
> Dramas are less interesting than movies.

❶ N보다 [bo·da] : than

▶ 보다 is a particle used to indicate comparison between two things.

▶ It's added after the subject or the object being compared.

❷ Rules

> It is irrelevant whether the noun ends with a vowel or a consonant.
>
> **공책 → 공책보다**   **고양이 → 고양이보다**
> than notebooks   than cats

You can change the positions of two objects.

책이 공책보다 비싸요. = 공책보다 책이 비싸요.
Books are more expensive than notebooks.

저는 고양이보다 강아지를 좋아해요. = 저는 강아지를 고양이보다 좋아해요.
I like dogs more than cats.

❸ 더 [deo] : more, 덜 [deol] : less

▶ 더 and 덜 are normally used together with 보다. 더 can be omitted.

▶ They are placed before the word that 'more' describes.

> 언니가 저보다 더 작아요. = 언니가 저보다 작아요.
> My sister is smaller than me.

> 어제보다 오늘이 덜 따뜻해.
> Today is less warm than yesterday.

✓
You can use 훨씬 [hwol·ssin] before 더 or 덜 to emphasize the comparison.
미국이 중국보다 훨씬 더 멀어요.
The United States is much further away than China.

WORDS   멀다 [meol·da] to be far   재미있다 [jae·mi·it·tta] to be fun

Master Grammar By Practicing!

A Arrange the given words appropriately.

🎧 10-02P.mp3

오빠가 (보다 / 더 / 언니 / 작아요)	→	오빠가 <u>언니보다 더 작아요.</u>

1. 콜라가 (보다 / 주스 / 시원해요 / 더) → 콜라가 _____
2. 서울이 (따뜻해요 / 보다 / 부산 / 덜) → 서울이 _____
3. 기차가 (더 / 보다 / 길어요 / 자동차) → 기차가 _____
4. 밥이 (덜 / 빵 / 보다 / 맛있어요) → 밥이 _____

B Change the positions of the underlined words so that the meaning remains the same.

<u>부산보다 서울이</u> 더 시원해요.	→	<u>서울이 부산보다</u> 더 시원해요.

1. <u>컴퓨터보다 핸드폰이</u> 더 비싸요. → _____ 더 비싸요.
2. 저는 <u>영화보다 드라마를</u> 더 좋아해요. → 저는 _____ 더 좋아해요.
3. <u>아빠보다 엄마가</u> 훨씬 더 작아요. → _____ 훨씬 더 작아요.
4. 저는 <u>커피보다 주스를</u> 더 자주 마셔요. → 저는 _____ 더 자주 마셔요.

C Look at the pictures and complete the sentences.

 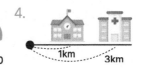

Q: 뭐가 더 비싸요? (아이스크림, 콜라)	A: <u>아이스크림이 콜라보다 더 비싸요.</u>

1. Q: 누가 더 작아요? (지수, 영미) A: _____
2. Q: 언제가 더 따뜻해요? (수요일, 목요일) A: _____
3. Q: 뭐가 더 싸요? (치마, 모자) A: _____
4. Q: 어디가 더 멀어요? (학교, 병원) A: _____

WORDS **시원하다** [si·won·ha·da] to be cool

UNIT 3 | 가장/제일 (the most), N중에서 (among) GRAMMAR

🎧 10-03G.mp3

> 롯데타워가 한국에서 제일 높아요.   저는 아이돌 중에서 **BTS**를 가장 좋아해요.
> Lotte Tower is the highest in Korea.   I like BTS the most among K-pop idols.

① 가장 [ga·jang] / 제일 [je·il] : the most, the best

▶ Both 가장 and 제일 are adverbs used in comparisons to express superlatives.

▶ You can use 가장 and 제일 interchangeably in everyday conversations.

저는 뉴진스를 제일 좋아해요.	I like New Jeans the most.
저는 한국어를 가장 잘해요.[1]	I speak Korean the best.

② N중에(서) [jung·e·seo] : among, between

▶ 중에 or 중에서[2] indicate a certain range of objects to choose from.

한국 음식 중에 뭐를 제일 좋아해요?
What do you like the most among Korean foods?

한국 드라마 중에서 <도깨비>가 제일 재미있어요.
Among Korean dramas, <Goblin> is the most interesting.

엄마랑 아빠 중에 누가 더 좋아요?
Between Mom and Dad, who do you like more?

▶ 에서 is used when choosing an object from a specific place.

유리가 학교에서 가장 작아요.
Yuri is the smallest in school.

[1] 잘 [hal] is an adverb that translates to 'well' in English.
잠을 잘 자요. I sleep well

It's also often used to express someone is doing something skillfully. In that case, 잘 and 하다(to do) are written together.
저는 요리를 잘해요.
I'm good at cooking.

[2] 중에 and 중에서 are interchangeable.

WORDS   높다 [nop·tta] to be high   잘 [jal] well   음식 [eum·sik] food

Master Grammar By Practicing!

 10-03P.mp3

A Rewrite the sentences using the expression of '가장' or '제일'.

> 저는 아이스크림을 좋아해요. → 저는 아이스크림을 가장 좋아해요.

1. 김치가 맛있어요. → _____

2. 오늘 날씨가 좋아요. → _____

3. 기차가 길어요. → _____

4. 저는 한국어를 자주 말해요. → _____

B Choose the correct option.

> 제니가 우리 회사(에서 / 중에서) 한국어를 가장 잘해요.

1. 저는 한국 음식 (에서 / 중에서) 비빔밥을 제일 좋아해요.

2. 아빠가 우리 가족 (에서 / 중에서) 요리를 가장 잘해요.

3. 피아노가 우리 집 (에서 / 중에서) 가장 비싸요.

4. 제주도가 한국 (에서 / 중에서) 가장 따뜻해요.

C Choose the correct option, either '에서' or '중에서' and fill in the blank using the given word.

> 헨리가 학교에서 수영을 가장 잘해요. (학교)
> 마리아가 우리 중에서 제일 작아요. (우리)

1. 민호가 _____ 제일 멋있어요. (제 친구)

2. 롯데타워가 _____ 가장 높아요. (한국)

3. 아이폰이 _____ 가장 비싸요. (핸드폰)

4. 피터가 _____ 일을 제일 잘해요. (회사)

WORDS 제주도 [je·ju·do] Jeju island   멋있다 [meo·sit·tta] to be cool, to be stylish

UNIT 4 | 무슨, 어떤, 어느 (what, which)

🎧 10-04G.mp3

어떤 음식을 좋아해요?
What kind of food do you like?

요즘 무슨 책을 읽어?
What book are you reading these days?

어떤, 무슨 and 어느 are question words used to inquire about nouns, but they are used in slightly different contexts.

> Rule: 어떤/무슨/어느 + Noun

① 어떤 [eo·tteon] : what kind of

▶ 어떤 is used when you want to inquire about the characteristics of something. It is used to ask about the type or kind of something.

Q: 어떤 영화를 좋아해요?   What kind of movies do you like?
A: 저는 코미디 영화를 좋아해요.   I like comedy movies.

② 무슨 [mu·seun] : what, which

▶ 무슨 is used when you want to inquire about a specific item among the existing options within a category.

Q: 무슨 노래를 제일 좋아해? What song do you like the most?[1]
A: 나는 BTS의 <봄날>을 제일 좋아해. I like BTS' <Spring Day> the most.

[1] Actual Meaning: What song do you like among the existing songs?

③ 어느 [eo·neu] : which

▶ 어느 is used to ask about a specific item or choice among several known options and implies a selection from a set of options. It's often used with locations.

Q: 어느 나라 사람이에요?   Which country are you from?
A: 저는 독일 사람이에요.   I'm German.

WORDS   나라 [na·ra] country

Master Grammar By Practicing!

🎧 10-04P.mp3

A Choose the appropriate question word.

Q: (어떤 / 무슨) 책을 읽어요?	A: <파친코>를 읽어요.

1. Q: (어떤 / 어느) 드라마를 좋아해요?　　A: 멜로 드라마를 좋아해요.
2. Q: (어느 / 어떤) 나라 사람이에요?　　A: 한국 사람이에요.
3. Q: 주말에 (어떤 / 무슨) 운동을 해요?　　A: 수영을 해요.
4. Q: (어떤 / 어느) 회사에 다녀요?　　A: 삼성에 다녀요.

B Fill in the blanks with the appropriate question word: '어느', '무슨', or '어떤'.

Q: 이건 <u>어느</u> 나라 음식이에요?	A: 그건 중국 음식이에요.

1. Q: 한국 음식 중에 _____ 음식을 제일 좋아해요?　　A: 비빔밥을 제일 좋아해요.
2. Q: _____ 자동차를 타요?　　A: BMW를 타요.
3. Q: _____ 자동차를 좋아해요?　　A: 클래식카를 좋아해요.
4. Q: 주로 _____ 카페에 가요?　　A: 주로 스타벅스에 가요.

C Complete the answer with the given word.

Q: 어느 나라 사람이에요? (독일)	A: <u>독일 사람이에요.</u>

1. Q: 어떤 영화를 싫어해요? (판타지)　　A: _____
2. Q: 무슨 음식이 맛있어요? (라면)　　A: _____
3. Q: 친구랑 어느 나라를 여행해요? (한국)　　A: _____
4. Q: 무슨 과일을 제일 좋아해요? (바나나)　　A: _____

WORDS

클래식카 [keul·rae·sik·ka] classic car　　　**스타벅스** [seu·ta·beok·seu] Starbucks
싫어하다 [si·reo·ha·da] to not like　　　**과일** [gwa·il] fruit

🎧 10-C.mp3

민호: 요코 씨는 영화 좋아해요? Do you like movies?

요코: 네, 정말 좋아해요. 그래서 자주 봐요.
Yes, I really like it. So I watch them often.

민호: 어떤 영화를 좋아해요? What kind of movies do you like?

요코: 저는 마블 영화 좋아해요. I like Marvel movies.

그 중에서 〈엔드 게임〉이 제일 재미있어요.
Among them, <End Game> is the most fun.

민호 씨는 주로 어떤 영화를 봐요.
What kind of movies do you usually watch?

민호: 저는 마블 영화보다 픽사를 더 좋아해요.
I like Pixar more than Marvel movies.

요코: 무슨 영화가 제일 좋아요? What movie do you like the most?

민호: 픽사 영화 중에서 저는 〈업〉이 제일 좋아요.
Among Pixar movies, I like <Up> the best.

NOTE

✏️ The expression 'I like something' can be conveyed in two different ways in Korean. One way is using the adjective '좋다(to be good),' and the other is using the verb '좋아하다(to like).' Therefore, '좋아하다' is used with an object, while '좋다' is used with a subject.

저는 영화를 좋아해요. = 저는 영화가 좋아요. = I like movies.

RECAP CHAPTER 10

❶ Conjugation of Korean Adjectives

If the last vowel of the word stem is ㅏ or ㅗ → word stem + 아요

If the last vowel of the word stem is neither ㅏ nor ㅗ → word stem + 어요

Every adjective with 하다 → 하다 changes to 해요

Statement	Question
A-아요 / A-어요 / 해요	A-아요? / A-어요? / 해요?
작아요 / 길어요 / 따뜻해요	작아요? / 길어요? / 따뜻해요?

❷ 어떻다: to be how

Formal polite	어떻습니까?
Informal polite	어때요?
Casual	어때?

❸ Comparative

보다: Particle indicating comparison (than)

더/덜: more/less

❹ Superlative

가장/제일: Adverb indicating the highest degree of something (the most)

중에(서):   Phrase indicating a certain range of objects to choose from (among)

❺ Difference between 어떤, 무슨 and 어느

어떤: When asking about the type or kind of something (what kind of)

무슨: When asking about a specific item among the existing options (what, which)

어느: When asking about a choice among several known options (which)

REVIEW TEST CHAPTER 10

A Choose the option that matches the verb and its conjugation correctly.

① 싸다 - 싸어요   ② 따뜻하다 - 따뜻하아요

③ 멀다 - 멀어요   ④ 높다 - 높어요

B Choose the **incorrect** sentence.

① 저는 아이스크림을 가장 좋아해요.

② 오늘이 어제보다 더 시원해요.

③ 제 컴퓨터보다 제니 컴퓨터가 비싸요.

④ 요즘 한국 드라마보다 제일 재미있어요.

C In the following passage, choose the option written **incorrectly**.

오늘 날씨가 아주 ①좋어요. 친구랑 같이 아이
스크림을 먹어요. 아이스크림이 정말 ②시원해
요. 그런데 아이스크림이 조금 ③비싸요. 하지
만 ④맛있어요.

D Choose the sentence where the underlined word is **incorrect**.

① 지수가 학교<u>에서</u> 가장 작아요.

② 한국 영화 <u>중에서</u> 뭐 제일 좋아해요?

③ 회사 <u>중에서</u> 누가 일을 제일 잘해요?

④ 친구 <u>중에</u> 누가 제일 좋아요?

E Choose the correct arrangement of the words in brackets.

I like Ramyeon the most among Korean foods.
(제일, 한국 음식, 라면을, 저는, 중에서) 좋아요.

① 저는 제일 한국 음식 중에서 라면을 좋아해요.

② 저는 한국 음식 중에서 라면을 제일 좋아해요.

③ 저는 제일 중에서 한국 음식 라면을 좋아해요.

④ 저는 라면을 중에서 한국 음식 제일 좋아해요.

F Choose the appropriate option for the blank space.

Q: _____ 영화를 제일 좋아해요.
A: <아바타>를 제일 좋아해요.
Q: _____ 나라를 여행해요?
A: 영국을 여행해요.

① 무슨 - 어느   ② 어떤 - 어느

③ 무슨 - 어떤   ④ 어떤 - 어떤

G Read the following phone call and choose the **incorrect** statement.

민호: 제니 씨, 미국은 날씨가 어때요?
제니: 여기는 날씨가 좋아요.
      한국은 어때요?
민호: 여기는 오늘 조금 흐려요.
      제니 씨는 요즘 뭐가 제일 맛있어요?
제니: 저는 한국 라면이 제일 맛있어요.
      민호 씨는요?
민호: 저는 요즘 과일만 먹어요.
      그런데 한국에서 과일이 너무 비싸요.

① 한국은 날씨가 흐립니다.

② 제니는 미국에 있습니다.

③ 제니는 라면이 제일 맛있습니다.

④ 민호는 과일을 먹지 않습니다.

🎧 10-V.mp3

No.	✓	Word	Meaning
1	☐	길다	
2	☐	높다	
3	☐	따뜻하다	
4	☐	맛있다	
5	☐	멀다	
6	☐	멋있다	
7	☐	비싸다	
8	☐	시원하다	
9	☐	싸다	
10	☐	작다	
11	☐	재미있다	
12	☐	좋다	
13	☐	흐리다	
14	☐	싫어하다	
15	☐	과일	
16	☐	음식	
17	☐	아이스크림	
18	☐	나라	
19	☐	날씨	
20	☐	제주도	
21	☐	잘	
22	☐	정말	
23	☐	조금	

It's time to review the new words you've learned in this chapter! Write down the meanings of the words and check the ones you have learned.

Number of words I've learned:

_____ / 23

Exploring Must-Try Korean Dishes ②

떡볶이 Tteokbokki

Tteokbokki is a spicy rice cake dish made by simmering rice cakes and fish cakes seasoned with 고추장 (red pepper paste) and 고춧가루 (red pepper flakes). It is a popular street food in Korea, widely enjoyed. A cherished national snack enjoyed by all ages, it holds a special place as a nostalgic dish from school days.

라면 Ramyeon

Ramyeon is a dish widely enjoyed in Korea for its convenience. It consists of noodles, a soup base, and additional ingredients such as meat and vegetables in the broth. Boil the noodles in water and add the soup base and ingredients to simmer together. It is typical to customize the dish by adding extra ingredients.

김밥 Kimbap

Kimbap is a dish made by rolling rice and various ingredients in seaweed. The rice is typically seasoned with salt and sesame oil to enhance its savory flavor. Various ingredients such as pickled radish, egg, vegetables, ham, fish cake, and beef are commonly used. Kimbap, being bite-sized and easy to eat with hands, is a popular choice for family outings.

치킨 Chicken

Korea's chicken culture boasts a variety of flavors and sauces, including the popular fried chicken, spiced chicken with spicy or soy-based sauces, and creatively topped options with cheese or vegetables. Enjoying chicken with beer, known as '치맥 (Chimaek)', is a prevalent social activity among adults.

CHAPTER 11
Irregular Conjugations

What you'll learn in this chapter

In the previous chapters, we covered regular conjugations. The regularity depends on whether the stem of the verb and adjective changes. Predicates whose stems change depending on the following suffix are called irregular verbs and adjectives. This chapter introduces four types of irregular conjugation. After completing this chapter, you will be able to use a more diverse range of verbs and adjectives.

🎧 11-01G.mp3

저는 오늘 많이 아파요.
I am very sick today.

제니가 친구에게 편지를 써요.
Jenny is writing a letter to her friend.

'—' Irregular Conjugation

If the word stem ends with —,

— is omitted + 아요 If the previous vowel is ㅏ or ㅗ
              어요 If the previous vowel is neither ㅏ nor ㅗ

아프다 to be sick → 아프 + 아요 → 아파요
word stem
the previous vowel is ㅏ   ommitted

Basic Form	-아/어요
크다 to be big	커요 [keo·yo]
예쁘다 to be pretty	예뻐요 [yeo·ppeo·yo]
바쁘다 to be busy	바빠요 [ba·ppa·yo]
아프다 to be sick	아파요 [a·pa·yo]
쓰다 to write	써요 [sseo·yo]

제 여동생이 저보다 키가 커요[1].
제니가 우리 학교에서 제일 예뻐요.
너 지금 바빠?

My younger sister is taller than me.
Jenny is the prettiest in our school.
Are you busy now?

[1] In Korean, there are no adjectives for height qualities. Instead, 크다 (to be big) and 작다 (to be small) with the word 키 (height) is used.

Therefore, 키가 크다 means 'to be tall', and 키가 작다 means 'to be short'.

WORDS
많이 [ma·ni] a lot, much   아프다 [a·peu·da] to be sick   쓰다 [sseu·da] to write
크다 [keu·da] to be big   예쁘다 [ye·ppeu·da] to be pretty   키 [ki] height
바쁘다 [ba·ppeu·da] to be busy

Master Grammar By Practicing!

 11-01P.mp3

A Change the ending form of the underlined words to '아/어요' form.

사과가 <u>크다</u>.	→	<u>사과가 커요</u>.

1. 아이가 정말 <u>예쁘다</u>.   →   _____
2. 선생님에게 이메일을 <u>쓰다</u>.   →   _____
3. 마리아가 요즘 너무 <u>바쁘다</u>.   →   _____
4. 오늘 날씨가 조금 <u>나쁘다</u>.   →   _____

B Correct the underlined words appropriately.

엄마, 지금 <u>바쁘요</u>?	→	엄마, 지금 <u>바빠요</u>?

1. 머리가 많이 <u>아퍼요</u>.   →   머리가 많이 _____
2. 헨리가 책을 <u>쓰어요</u>.   →   헨리가 책을 _____
3. 저는 오늘 조금 <u>슬파요</u>.   →   저는 오늘 조금 _____
4. 제니의 집이 정말 <u>크요</u>.   →   제니의 집이 정말 _____

C Choose the corresponding word and change the ending form to '아/어요' form.

아프다   바쁘다   나쁘다   슬프다   쓰다

오늘은 부모님의 생일이에요. 그래서 부모님에게 편지를 <u>써요</u>.

1. 내일이 시험이에요. 그래서 저는 오늘 많이 _____
2. 오늘은 날씨가 정말 안 좋아요. 날씨가 _____
3. 요즘 남자친구를 못 만나요. 그래서 너무 _____
4. 오늘 공부를 너무 많이 해요. 그래서 머리가 _____

WORDS

너무 [neo·mu] too, so
나쁘다 [na·ppeu·da] to be bad

머리 [meo·ri] head
슬프다 [seul·peu·da] to be sad

UNIT 2 'ㅂ' Conjugation

11-02G.mp3

> 요즘 날씨가 더워요.
> The weather is hot these days.
>
> 저는 치마를 자주 입어요.
> I wear skirts often.

'ㅂ' Irregular Conjugation

If the word stem ends with ㅂ,

ㅂ changes to 우 + 어요 → 워요

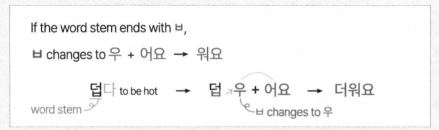

덥다 to be hot → 덥 우 + 어요 → 더워요
word stem   ㅂ changes to 우

Basic Form	-아/어요
덥다 to be hot	더워요 [deo·wo·yo]
어렵다 to be difficult	어려워요 [eo·ryeo·wo·yo]
귀엽다 to be cute	귀여워요 [gwi·yeo·wo·yo]
돕다 to help	도와요 [do·wa·yo][1]

[1] 돕다 is an exceptional word that changes to 와요 instead of 워요.

제 친구의 아기가 정말 귀여워요. My friend's baby is really cute.
한국어가 영어보다 더 어려워요. Korean is more difficult than English.

'ㅂ' Regular Conjugation

Some verbs and adjectives ending with ㅂ are conjugated regularly.

Basic Form	-아/어요
입다 to wear	입어요 [i·beo·yo]
좁다 to be narrow	좁아요 [jo·ba·yo]

저는 오늘 치마를 입어요. I wear a skirt today.
저 길은 너무 좁아요. That road is too narrow.

WORDS
덥다 [deop·tta] to be hot	입다 [ip·tta] to wear	귀엽다 [gwi·yeop·tta] to be cute
어렵다 [eo·ryeop·tta] to be difficult	길 [gil] road, street	좁다 [jop·tta] to be narrow

Master Grammar By Practicing!

🎧 11-02P.mp3

A Choose the correct option.

> 제니의 고양이가 아주 (귀엽어요 / 귀여워요).

1. 한국의 1월은 정말 (추와요 / 추워요).
2. 민호가 엄마의 일을 (도워요 / 도와요).
3. 저는 주로 치마를 (입어요 / 이워요).
4. 한국 음식은 보통 많이 (맵어요 / 매워요).

B Correct the underlined words appropriately.

> 제 가방이 오빠 가방보다 <u>무겁어요</u>.   →   제 가방이 오빠 가방보다 <u>무거워요</u>.

1. 제 핸드폰이 정말 <u>가벼와요</u>.   →   제 핸드폰이 정말 _____
2. 떡볶이가 아주 <u>맵어요</u>.   →   떡볶이가 아주 _____
3. 제니가 아침에 옷을 <u>입워요</u>.   →   제니가 아침에 옷을 _____
4. 영어 시험이 <u>쉬와요</u>.   →   영어 시험이 _____

C Choose the corresponding word and change the ending form to '아/어요' form.

덥다	어렵다	춥다	귀엽다	돕다

> 저는 요즘 한국어를 공부해요. 그런데 한국어가 너무 <u>어려워요</u>.

1. 지금 친구의 아기를 만나요. 아기가 정말 _____
2. 한국은 지금 8월이에요. 그래서 날씨가 너무 _____
3. 엄마가 부엌에서 많이 바빠요. 그래서 아빠가 엄마를 _____
4. 창문을 열어요. 그래서 방이 조금 _____

WORDS

춥다 [chup·tta] to be cold   **돕다** [dop·tta] to help   **맵다** [meap·tta] to be spicy
무겁다 [mu·geop·tta] to be heavy   **가볍다** [ga·byeop·tta] to be light   **쉽다** [swip·tta] to be easy

UNIT 3 | 'ㄷ' Conjugation

🎧 11-03G.mp3

> 저는 자주 음악을 들어요.
> I often listen to music.

> 엄마가 창문을 닫아요.
> My mom is closing the window.

'ㄷ' Irregular Conjugation

If the word stem ends with ㄷ,

ㄷ changes to ㄹ +
- 아요 If the previous vowel is ㅏ or ㅗ
- 어요 If the previous vowel is neither ㅏ nor ㅗ

듣다 to hear → 듣 → ㄹ + 어요 → 들어요

word stem ↲   The previous vowel   ㄷ changes to ㄹ
of stem is neither ㅏ nor ㅗ

Basic Form	-아/어요
듣다 to listen	들어요 [deu·reo·yo]
걷다 to walk	걸어요 [geo·reo·yo]
묻다 to ask	물어요 [mu·reo·yo]

친구랑 같이 학교까지 걸어요.   I walk to school with my friends.
다니엘은 선생님에게 자주 물어요.   Daniel often asks his teacher.

'ㄷ' Regular Conjugation

Some verbs and adjectives ending with ㄷ are conjugated regularly.

Basic Form	-아/어요
닫다 to close	닫아요 [da·da·yo]
받다 to receive	받아요 [ba·da·yo]

제니에게 생일 선물을 받아요.   I receive a birthday present from Jenny.

WORDS

음악 [eu·mak] music   듣다 [deut·tta] to hear, to listen (to)   닫다 [dat·tta] to close
걷다 [geot·tta] to walk   묻다 [mut·tta] to ask

Master Grammar By Practicing!

🎧 11-03P.mp3

A Choose the correct option.

> 공원에서 자주 길을 (걷어요 / 걸어요).

1. 회사에서 매일 이메일을 (발아요 / 받아요).
2. 핸드폰으로 팟캐스트를 (듣어요 / 들어요).
3. 제니가 콜라 병을 (닫아요 / 달아요).
4. 프랑스 사람에게 길을 (물어요 / 묻어요).

B Change the ending form of the underlined words to '아/어요' form.

> 친구랑 같이 BTS 음악을 <u>듣다</u>.   →   친구랑 같이 BTS 음악을 <u>들어요</u>.

1. 아이가 창문을 <u>닫다</u>   →   아이가 창문을 _____
2. 집에서 학교까지 <u>걷다</u>.   →   집에서 학교까지 _____
3. 엄마가 전화를 <u>받다</u>.   →   엄마가 전화를 _____
4. 제니에게 시간을 <u>묻다</u>.   →   제니에게 시간을 _____

C Choose the corresponding word and change the ending form to '아/어요' form.

> 듣다   걷다   닫다   받다   묻다

> 날씨가 너무 추워요. 그래서 창문을 <u>닫아요</u>.

1. 저는 운동을 안 해요. 하지만 매일 한 시간 _____
2. 오늘은 제 생일이에요. 그래서 선물을 많이 _____
3. 저는 핸드폰이 없어요. 그래서 헨리에게 시간을 _____
4. 저는 케이팝을 좋아해요. 그래서 노래를 매일 _____

WORDS   팟캐스트 [pat·kae·seu·teu] podcast

 11-04G.mp3

한국어와 영어는 많이 달라요.
Korean and English are very different.

저는 노래를 잘 불러요.
I sing well.

'르' Irregular Conjugation

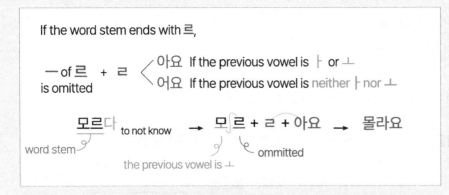

If the word stem ends with 르,

一 of 르 + ㄹ
is omitted

아요 If the previous vowel is ㅏ or ㅗ
어요 If the previous vowel is neither ㅏ nor ㅗ

모르다 to not know → 모 르 + ㄹ + 아요 → 몰라요
word stem

the previous vowel is ㅗ   ommitted

Basic Form	-아/어요
다르다 to be different	달라요 [dal·la·yo]
빠르다 to be fast	빨라요 [ppal·la·yo]
모르다 to not know	몰라요 [mol·la·yo]
부르다 to call, to sing	불러요 [bul·leo·yo]
고르다 to choose	골라요 [gol·la·yo]

저는 그 사람을 잘 몰라요.
I don't know that person very well.

비행기가 기차보다 훨씬 더 빨라요.
Planes are much faster than trains.

저는 친구랑 같이 한국 식당에서 음식을 골라요.
I'm choosing food at a Korean restaurant with my friend.

Master Grammar By Practicing!

🎧 11-04P.mp3

A Choose the correct option.

> 자동차가 자전거보다 (빠르어요 / 빨라요).

1. 할머니가 할아버지를 (불러요 / 불어요).
2. 제 남자친구는 한국을 잘 (몰라요 / 몰러요).
3. 저와 제 동생은 너무 (다르어요 / 달라요).
4. 옷가게에서 옷을 (골라요 / 골러요).

B Correct the underlined words appropriately.

> 독일 사과와 한국 사과는 <u>다르어요</u>.　　→　　독일 사과와 한국 사과는 <u>달라요</u>.

1. 제니 씨는 무슨 음식을 <u>골아요</u>?　　→　　제니 씨는 무슨 음식을 ＿＿＿＿＿＿＿＿
2. 다니엘은 한국 드라마를 잘 <u>모르아요</u>.　　→　　다니엘은 한국 드라마를 잘 ＿＿＿＿＿＿＿＿
3. 집에서 회사까지 자전거가 제일 <u>빨러요</u>　　→　　집에서 회사까지 자전거가 제일 ＿＿＿＿＿＿＿＿
4. 선생님과 학생이 함께 노래를 <u>부르어요</u>.　　→　　선생님과 학생이 함께 노래를 ＿＿＿＿＿＿＿＿

C Choose the corresponding word and change the ending form to '아/어요' form.

> 부르다　　　빠르다　　　고르다　　　다르다　　　모르다

> 제 동생이 저보다 키가 작아요. 그런데 동생이 저보다 더 <u>빨라요</u>.

1. 오늘은 제 생일이에요. 그래서 저는 노래를 ＿＿＿＿＿＿＿＿
2. 저는 고양이 한 마리와 개 한 마리가 있어요. 그런데 고양이와 개는 많이 ＿＿＿＿＿＿＿＿
3. 내일은 제니의 생일이에요. 그래서 백화점에서 선물을 ＿＿＿＿＿＿＿＿
4. 저는 텔레비전을 안 봐요. 그래서 드라마를 잘 ＿＿＿＿＿＿＿＿

🎧 11-C.mp3

제니: 민호 씨, 한국은 날씨가 어때요? Minho, how is the weather in Korea?

민호: 여기는 요즘 날씨가 따뜻해요. The weather is warm here these days.

거기는 어때요? How about there?

제니: 미국은 요즘 조금 추워요. It's a little cold in America these days.

민호: 제니 씨는 요즘도 한국어 공부 많이 해요?
Are you also studying Korean a lot these days?

제니: 아니요, 많이 못 해요. No, I can't do much.

한국어는 너무 어려워요. Korean is too difficult.

그런데 한국 음식은 자주 먹어요. But I eat Korean food often.

민호: 한국 음식은 제니한테 너무 맵지 않아요?
Isn't Korean food too spicy for you?

제니: 조금 매워요. 하지만 정말 맛있어요.
It's a little spicy. But it's really delicious.

WORDS   하지만 [ha·ji·man] however, but

RECAP CHAPTER 11

❶ '一' Irregular Conjugation

If the word stem ends with 一 → 一 is omitted
→ if the previous vowel is ㅏ or ㅗ → 아요
→ if the previous vowel is neither ㅏ nor ㅗ → 어요

아프다	예쁘다	쓰다
아파요	예뻐요	써요

❷ 'ㅂ' Irregular Conjugation

If the word stem ends with ㅂ → ㅂ changes to 우
→ 우 + 어요 → 워요

쉽다	덥다	무겁다
쉬워요	더워요	무거워요

Regular Conjugation	
입다	좁다
입어요	좁아요

❸ 'ㄷ' Irregular Conjugation

If the word stem ends with ㄷ → ㄷ changed to ㄹ
→ if the previous vowel is ㅏ or ㅗ → 아요
→ if the previous vowel is neither ㅏ nor ㅗ → 어요

듣다	걷다	묻다
들어요	걸어요	물어요

Regular Conjugation	
닫다	받다
닫아요	받아요

❹ '르' Irregular Conjugation

If the word stem ends with 르 → 一 of 르 is omitted + ㄹ
→ if the previous vowel is ㅏ or ㅗ → 아요
→ if the previous vowel is neither ㅏ nor ㅗ → 어요

모르다	다르다	부르다
몰라요	달라요	불러요

REVIEW TEST CHAPTER 11

A Choose the option that matches the verb and conjugation **incorrectly**.

① 나쁘다 - 나뻐요　　② 예쁘다 - 예뻐요

③ 크다 - 커요　　④ 슬프다 - 슬퍼요

B Choose the correct conjugation of the underlined verb in informal polite form.

> 저는 BTS의 노래를 <u>부르다</u>.
> 친구의 생일 선물을 <u>고르다</u>.

① 부르어요 - 고르아요

② 부르어요 - 골라요

③ 불러요 - 골라요

④ 불러요 - 고르아요

C Choose the correct sentence.

① 제 여자친구는 정말 귀엽어요.

② 마리아는 옷을 잘 이워요.

③ 김치가 라면보다 더 맵어요.

④ 우리 집은 너무 좁아요.

D Choose the verb or adjective that follows regular conjugation

① 듣다　　② 걷다

③ 받다　　④ 묻다

E In the following passage, choose the option with the **incorrectly** conjugated verb.

> 헨리는 요즘 아주 ①바쁘어요. 그런데 오늘 헨리가 ②아파요. 그래서 헨리가 제니를 ③불러요. 제니가 헨리의 일을 ④도와요.

F Choose the sentence where the underlined word is **incorrect**.

① 뭐가 제일 <u>가벼워요</u>?

② 영어와 한국어가 많이 <u>달라요</u>?

③ 서울이랑 부산 중에 어디가 더 <u>덥어요</u>?

④ 다니엘이 그 사람을 <u>몰라요</u>?

G Read the following dialogue and choose the **incorrect** statement.

> 제니: 저는 오늘 가방을 사요.
> 　　　수지 씨는 어떤 옷 사요?
> 수지: 저는 치마를 사요.
> 제니: 이 치마 어때요?
> 수지: 그 치마 너무 예뻐요.
> 　　　그런데 너무 비싸요.
> 　　　제니 씨, 이 가방은 어때요?
> 제니: 그 가방 정말 귀여워요.
> 　　　그리고 가벼워요.
> 　　　그런데 이 가방도 너무 비싸요.
> 　　　그래서 안 사요.

① 제니와 수지가 쇼핑을 합니다.

② 치마가 수지에게 비쌉니다.

③ 가방이 제니에게 예쁩니다.

④ 제니는 가방을 사지 않습니다.

🎧 11-V.mp3

No.	✓	Word	Meaning	No.	✓	Word	Meaning
1	☐	가볍다		18	☐	걷다	
2	☐	귀엽다		19	☐	고르다	
3	☐	나쁘다		20	☐	닫다	
4	☐	다르다		21	☐	돕다	
5	☐	덥다		22	☐	듣다	
6	☐	맵다		23	☐	모르다	
7	☐	무겁다		24	☐	묻다	
8	☐	바쁘다		25	☐	부르다	
9	☐	빠르다		26	☐	쓰다	
10	☐	쉽다		27	☐	입다	
11	☐	슬프다		28	☐	길	
12	☐	아프다		29	☐	머리	
13	☐	어렵다		30	☐	음악	
14	☐	예쁘다		31	☐	키	
15	☐	좁다		32	☐	너무	
16	☐	춥다		33	☐	많이	
17	☐	크다		34	☐	하지만	

Number of words
I've learned:

_____ / 34

Exploring the masterpieces of film director Bong Joon-ho

Director Bong Joon-ho experienced a historic moment at the 92nd Academy Awards with his film '기생충 (Parasite)', winning in four categories including Best Picture and Best Director. Bong Joon-ho's films are known for their genre-blending narratives, social commentary, and masterful storytelling. Here are the representative works of Director Bong Joon-ho.

살인의 추억 Memories of Murder (2003)
Based on real events, it follows two detectives as they investigate a series of brutal murders in a small town. The film skillfully combines tension, dark humor, and social commentary, highlighting the impact of the crimes on both the victims and investigators. Bong's atmospheric storytelling and the outstanding performances of the cast contribute to the film's status as a critically acclaimed masterpiece.

괴물 The Host (2006)
The story centers on a dysfunctional family's quest to rescue their daughter from a mutated creature that emerges from the Han River. Blending horror, drama, and dark comedy, the film skillfully explores societal and environmental themes, delivering thrilling monster sequences.

설국열차 Snowpiercer (2013)
Set aboard a train carrying the last survivors of a frozen Earth, the film follows a rebellion led by passengers from the train's lower class. Exploring social inequality and class struggle, the movie cleverly uses the train's compartments as a metaphor for societal divisions. With intense action sequences and a thought-provoking narrative, "Snowpiercer" marks Bong's English-language debut.

기생충 Parasite (2019)
It explores social inequality through the story of the Kim family, who manipulate their way into the lives of the wealthy Park family. The film masterfully blends dark comedy, thriller, and drama, offering a sharp critique of class struggle and economic disparity. "Parasite" is celebrated not only for its success but also for its impact on discussions around social issues and the global recognition it brought to Korean cinema.

- Answers

- Index of Grammar

- Index of Vocabulary

Chapter 0 Learning Hangeul

Unit 1 한글: Introducing Hangeul   p. 11

A 1. vowel   2. consonant   3. consonant
  4. vowel   5. vowel

B 1. incorrect   2. correct   3. correct
  4. incorrect   5. correct

C 1. 매   2. 초   3. 남
  4. 흰   5. 족

Unit 2 모음 1: Basic Vowels   p. 13

A 1. 유   2. 어   3. 우
  4. 이   5. 여

B 1. 아이   2. 이
  3. 오이   4. 여우

C 1. 우유   2. 여우
  3. 이   4. 오이

Unit 3 자음 1: Basic Consonant   p. 15

A 1. 바   2. 타   3. 다
  4. 차   5. 가

B 1. 모자   2. 지도   3. 나무
  4. 비누   5. 치마

C 1. 커피   2. 바나나
  3. 치마   4. 기차

Unit 4 모음 2: Complex Vowels   p. 17

A 1. 애   2. 봐   3. 귀
  4. 네   5. 줘

B 1. 개   2. 화가   3. 가게
  4. 카메라 5. 시계

C 1. 테니스 2. 개
  3. 사과   4. 노래

Unit 5 자음 2: Double Consonants   p. 19

A 1. 쭈   2. 뽀   3. 끼
  4. 쓰   5. 때

B 1. 쓰다   2. 뿌리   3. 비싸다
  4. 찌르다 5. 끄다

C 1. 예쁘다 2. 싸다
  3. 토끼   4. 아빠

Unit 6 받침: Final Consonants   p. 21

A 1. 긴   2. 방   3. 꼭
  4. 말   5. 숲

B 1. 꽃   2. 먹다   3. 밥
  4. 몸   5. 손

C 1. 책   2. 옷
  3. 꽃   4. 듣다

Chapter 1 Characteristics of Korean

Unit 1 Korean Sentence Structure   p. 25

A 1. 와요   2. 읽어요   3. 가요
  4. 공부해요 5. 사요

B 1. 가   2. 이   3. 가
  4. 이   5. 가

C 1. 을   2. 를   3. 를
  4. 을   5. 를

Unit 2 Conjugation of Verbs and Adjectives   p. 27

A 1. 다   2. 다   3. 다
  4. 다   5. 다

B 1. 먹   2. 마시   3. 사
  4. 작   5. 따뜻하

C 1. 먹었습니다 2. 작으셨어   3. 따뜻했어요
  4. 마시세요   5. 잡니다

Unit 3 Korean Speech Style: 존댓말/반말   p. 29

A 1. 마십니다 2. 좋습니다   3. 일합니다
  4. 봅니다   5. 따뜻합니다

B 1. 먹어요   2. 따뜻해요   3. 읽어요
  4. 예뻐요   5. 사요

C 1. 작아 2. 마셔 3. 사
  4. 좋아 5. 예뻐

Unit 4 Numbers in Korean   p. 31

A 1. 칠십사 2. 팔만 이천
  3. 이백칠십육 4. 오십사만 천이백삼십

B 1. 열일곱 2. 스물아홉
  3. 서른여섯 4. 마흔하나

Chapter 2 "Be" Verb

Unit 1 N이다 (to be verb)   p. 35

A 1. 이에요 2. 이에요
  3. 이에요 4. 예요

B 1. 입니다 / 예요 / 야 2. 입니다 / 이에요 / 이야
  3. 입니다 / 예요 / 야 4. 입니다 / 이에요 / 이야

C 1. incorrect, 입니다 2. correct
  3. incorrect, 예요 4. incorrect, 이에요

Unit 2 N은/는 (topic particle)   p. 37

A 1. 는 2. 은
  3. 는 4. 는

B 1. incorrect, 는 2. correct
  3. incorrect, 는 4. incorrect, 는

C 1. 은, 동생은 학생이야. 2. 는, 저는 미국 사람입니다.
  3. 는, 아버지는 선생님이에요. 4. 는, 엄마는 의사야

Unit 3 Questioning with 'N이다'   p. 39

A 1. 예요 2. 이에요
  3. 야 4. 이야

B 1. 아니요 2. 네
  3. 아니요 4. 아니요

C 1. 아니 2. 아니
  3. 응 4. 응

Unit 4 N이/가 아니다 (to not be)   p. 41

A 1. 가 아닙니다 2. 이 아니에요
  3. 이 아니에요 4. 이 아니야

B 1. 이 아닙니다 / 이 아니에요 / 이 아니야
  2. 가 아닙니다 / 가 아니에요 / 가 아니야
  3. 가 아닙니다 / 가 아니에요 / 가 아니야
  4. 이 아닙니다 / 이 아니에요 / 이 아니야

C 1. 대학생이 아니에요. 2. 한국 사람이 아니야.
  3. 의사가 아닙니다. 4. 배우가 아니에요.

REVIEW TEST   p. 44

A ③ 이

B ② singer - 배우 (→ 가수)

C ③ 동생은 학생이 아니에요.

D ② 오빠, 언니

E ④ 아니요

F ③ 회사원

G ② 제니는 한국 사람이 아닙니다.

VOCABULARY   p. 45

1. Korea 2. USA
3. Germany 4. person
5. student 6. college student
7. teacher 8. singer
9. actor, actress 10. doctor
11. office worker 12. mother
13. mom 14. father
15. dad 16. older sister for girls
17. older brother for girls 18. older sister for boys
19. older brother for boys 20. younger brother/sister
21. younger brother 22. younger sister

Chapter 3 Indicating an Object

Unit 1 이것, 그것, 저것 (this, that, that)   p. 49

A 1. 그것   2. 이것, 그것
  3. 이것, 저것   4. 저것

B 1. 이것은 / 이건 / 이거   2. 그것은 / 그건 / 그거
  3. 저것은 / 저건 / 저거   4. 그것은 / 그건 / 그거

Unit 2 무엇 (what)   p. 51

A 1. 뭐예요?   2. 무엇입니까?
  3. 뭐야?   4. 뭐예요?

B 1. 그건 뭐예요?   2. 저건 뭐야?
  3. 이건 뭐야?   4. 저건 뭐예요?

C 1. 이거 뭐예요?   2. 그거 뭐예요?
  3. 저거 뭐야?   4. 저거 뭐예요?

Unit 3 N의 (of)   p. 53

A 1. 엄마의   2. 다니엘의
  3. 할아버지의   4. 아이의

B 1. 엄마의 우산이에요.   2. 여동생의 모자예요.
  3. 할머니의 공책이에요.   4. 아이의 치마예요.

C 1. 다니엘 가방이 아니에요.   2. 친구 책이 아니야.
  3. 언니 치마가 아니에요.   4. 할아버지 자동차가 아니야.

REVIEW TEST   p. 56

A ② 저거

B ④ notebook - 연필 (→ 공책)

C ② 그거 책의 친구야.
    (→ 그거 친구의 책이야. That is my friend's book.)

D ① 무엇이에요? → 뭐예요?

E ③ 할아버지의 의자

F ③ The camera belongs to Lisa's dad. (→ older sister)

G ④ 이거 - 아니요 - 저건

VOCABULARY   p. 57

1. book   2. notebook

3. pencil   4. picture, painting

5. umbrella   6. bag

7. clothes   8. shoes

9. hat   10. skirt

11. flower   12. tree

13. cellphone   14. camera

15. computer   16. television

17. car   18. grandfather

19. grandmother   20. friend

21. child   22. Nam mountain

23. Korean (language)

Chapter 4   Indicating Location

Unit 1 N이/가 있다(there is/to have) & N에(at/in) p. 61

A 1. 가   2. 이
  3. 가   4. 이

B 1. 자동차가 없어요.   2. 여동생이 있어.
  3. 집이 없어.   4. 카메라가 있습니다.

C 1. 방에 칠판이 있어요.   2. 커피숍에 책이 없어요.
  3. 방에 침대가 없어.   4. 교실에 컴퓨터가 있어.

Unit 2 여기,거기,저기(here, there) & 어디(where) p. 63

A 1. 도서관입니다.   2. 병원이야.
  3. 식당이에요.

B 1. 거기   2. 저기
  3. 여기

C 1. 어디예요?   2. 어디에 있어요?
  3. 어디에 있어요?   4. 어디예요?

Unit 3 Positional Words   p. 65

A 1. e   2. d
  3. a   4. b

B 1. 자동차가 집 사이에   2. 칠판이 책상 뒤에
  3. 창문 앞에 컵이   4. 가방 안에 고양이가

C 1. 옆에 있어요.   2. 뒤에 있어요.
  3. 위에 있어요.   4. 아래(or 밑)에 있어요.

REVIEW TEST   p. 68

A ① 이-가

B ③ 엄마는 자동차가 있어요.

C ② 어디예요?

D ① in front of - 옆 (→ 앞)

E ② 나무가 창문 밖에 있어요.

F ③ 교실에 컴퓨터가 없습니다.
    (→ 교실에 컴퓨터가 있습니다.)

VOCABULARY   p. 69

1. house	2. school
3. library	4. bookstore
5. hospital	6. bank
7. restaurant	8. cafe
9. coffee shop	10. park
11. mountain	12. sea
13. room	14. living room
15. classroom	16. bed
17. desk	18. chair
19. piano	20. black board
21. window	22. box
23. cup	24. cat
25. and	

Chapter 5 Personal Pronouns

Unit 1 저/나 (I), 저희/우리 (we)   p. 73

A 1. 나는   2. 우리는
   3. 저는   4. 저희는

B 1. 저희는   2. 우리는
   3. 나는   4. 저는

C 1. correct   2. incorrect, 나는
   3. incorrect, 저는   4. incorrect, 우리는

Unit 2 당신/너 (you)   p. 75

A 1. 너   2. 너
   3. 너희들   4. 너희들

B 1. 너는   2. 선생님은
   3. 지수는   4. 선생님은

C 1. 제니 씨는   2. -
   3. 너희들은   4. -

Unit 3 그분, 그 사람 (he/she) & 누구 (who)   p. 77

A 1. 이분   2. 저분
   3. 그분   4. 저분

B 1. 이분은   2. 얘는
   3. 이 사람은   4. 이분은

C 1. 누구야?   2. 누구예요?
   3. 누구야?   4. 누구예요?

Unit 4 Possessive Pronouns & 누구의 (whose) p. 79

A 1. 내   2. 우리
   3. 제   4. 제

B 1. incorrect, 네   2. incorrect, 네
   3. correct   4. incorrect, 내

C 1. 제   2. 우리
   3. 저희   4. 네

REVIEW TEST   p. 82

A ② 제

B ① 저희는 배우예요.

C ③ 이분들은 우리의 부모님이야.

D ④ 그것은 제 친구의 가방이에요.

E ③ 그 사람 (→ 그분)

F ② 유나의 남동생은 여자친구가 있습니다.
    (→ 유나의 남동생은 여자친구가 없습니다.)

VOCABULARY p. 83

1. family	2. parents
3. husband	4. wife
5. daughter	6. son
7. baby	8. woman
9. man	10. boss, CEO
11. France	12. China
13. name	14. occupation, job
15. hobby	16. swimming
17. shopping	18. company
19. movie actor	20. glasses
21. picture, photo	22. then

Chapter 6 Expressing Actions

Unit 1 V-(스)ㅂ니다 p. 87

A 1. 먹습니다 2. 일합니다
  3. 쉽니다 4. 앉습니다

B 1. correct 2. incorrect, 잡니까?
  3. incorrect, 공부합니까? 4. correct

C 1. 엄마가 일합니다. 2. 제니가 잡니다.
  3. 친구가 앉습니다. 4. 할머니가 쉽니다.

Unit 2 N을/를 (object particle) & 무엇을 (what) p. 89

A 1. 를 2. 을
  3. 을 4. 를

B 1. 을 2. 를
  3. 를 4. 을

C 1. 제니가 책을 읽습니다.
  2. 아빠가 빵을 먹습니다.
  3. 동생이 쇼핑을 좋아합니다.
  4. 아들이 한국어를 공부합니다.

Unit 3 V-아요/-아 & N에 p. 91

A 2. 라 - ㄷ - e 3. 마 - ㄹ - a
  4. 다 - ㄴ - d 5. 가 - ㅁ - b

B 1. 살아요 2. 자요
  3. 앉아요 4. 만나요

C 1. 학교에 와요. 2. 식당에 가요.
  3. 의자에 앉아요. 4. 자동차에 타요.

Unit 4 V-어요/-어 & N에서 p. 93

A 1. 마셔요 2. 먹어요
  3. 가르쳐요 4. 쉬어요

B 1. 줘요 / 줘 2. 가르쳐요 / 가르쳐
  3. 읽어요 / 읽어 4. 배워요 / 배워
  5. 마셔요 / 마셔

C 1. 학교에서 한국어를 배워요.
  2. 도서관에서 책을 읽어요.
  3. 교실에서 콜라를 마셔요.
  4. 미국에서 한국어를 가르쳐요.

Unit 5 하다 Verbs & 누가 (who) p. 95

A 2. 가 - ㄱ - d 3. 다 - ㅁ - b
  4. 마 - ㄷ - e 5. 라 - ㄴ - a

B 1. 누가 2. 누구의
  3. 누구를 4. 누가

C 1. 누구예요 2. 누가
  3. 누구의 4. 누구를

REVIEW TEST p. 98

A ③ 앉다 - 앉어요 (→ 앉아요)

B ① 을 - 를

C ③ 일합니다 - 앉습니다

D ② 친구가 한국어를 배우아요.
    (→ 친구가 한국어를 배워요.)

E ③ 카페에 (→ 카페에서)

F ④ 누구 한국어를 가르쳐요? (→ 누가)

G ③ 민호는 제니를 만납니다.
    (→ 수지는 제니를 만납니다.)

VOCABULARY

p. 99

1. to go
2. to teach
3. to drink
4. to meet
5. to eat
6. to learn
7. to see, to watch
8. to live
9. to rest
10. to sit
11. to come
12. to read
13. to sleep
14. to give
15. to get in, to ride
16. to study
17. to love
18. to cook
19. to exercise
20. to work
21. drama
22. to like
23. rice
24. bread
25. cola

Chapter 7 Negative Sentences

Unit 1 안 V, V-지 않다 (do not) p. 103

A 2. 마 - d   3. 나 - a
   4. 라 - e   5. 가 - c

B 1. 안 먹어요.   2. 안 자요.
   3. 안 삽니다.   4. 안 배워.

C 1. 가르치지 않아요.   2. 씻지 않아.
   3. 보지 않아요.   4. 사지 않습니다.

Unit 2 못 V, V-지 못하다 (cannot) p. 105

A 2. 가 - c   3. 라 - b
   4. 마 - a   5. 다 - e

B 1. 못 일어나요.   2. 못 쉬어요.
   3. 못 마셔.   4. 못 탑니다.

C 1. 가지 못해요.   2. 배우지 못해.
   3. 먹지 못합니다. 4. 오지 못해요.

Unit 3 Negation of 하다 Verbs p. 107

A 1. 공부를 안 해요. / 공부하지 않아요.
   2. 운전을 안 해. / 운전하지 않아.
   3. 노래를 안 해요. / 노래하지 않아요.
   4. 요리를 안 합니다. / 요리하지 않습니다.

B 1. 운전을 못 해요. / 운전하지 못해요.
   2. 요리를 못 해요. / 요리하지 못해요.
   3. 청소를 못 해. / 청소하지 못해.
   4. 노래를 못 합니다. / 노래하지 못합니다.

C 1. incorrect, 저는 오늘 쇼핑을 안 해요../
      저는 오늘 쇼핑하지 않아요.
   2. incorrect, 제니가 요리를 못 해요./
      제니가 요리하지 못해요.
   3. correct
   4. incorrect, 우리는 매일 청소를 안 해./
      우리는 매일 청소하지 않아.

REVIEW TEST p. 110

A ② 안 - 마시지

B ④ to cook - 운동하다 (→ 요리하다)

C ① I don't drive. - 안 운전해요.
      (→ 운전 안 해요. / 운전하지 않아요.)

D ④ 사지 못합니다 - 씻지 않습니다

E ③ 제 여동생은 집에서 요리를 안 해요.

F ③ 지수의 언니는 일을 합니다.
      (→ 지수의 언니는 일을 하지 않습니다.)

VOCABULARY p. 111

1. to buy
2. to wash
3. to open
4. to get up
5. to sing
6. to take a shower
7. to drive
8. to clean up
9. to have a party
10. meat
11. banana
12. apple
13. water
14. drink, alcohol
15. milk
16. coffee
17. hand
18. bicycle
19. every day
20. today

21. these days　　　　　　22. early

23. often　　　　　　　　24. now

25. so, therefore

Chapter 8　Expressing Numbers

Unit 1　Counting & 몇 (how many)　　　p. 115

A　1. 한　　　　　　　　2. 열 세
　　3. 네　　　　　　　　4. 스무

B　1. 네 마리　　　　　　2. 열두 명
　　3. 일곱 권　　　　　　4. 두 잔

C　1. 스물다섯 살　　　　2. 열한 분
　　3. 다섯 병　　　　　　4. 세 잔

Unit 2　Telling Time　　　p. 117

A　2. a　　　　　　　　3. e
　　4. b　　　　　　　　5. c

B　1. 네 시 반　　　　　　2. 세 시 오 분 전
　　3. 아홉 시 반　　　　　4. 열두 시 십 분 전

C　1. 열 시입니다.　　　　2. 몇 시야?
　　3. 몇 시예요?　　　　　4. 세 시 십오 분이에요.

Unit 3　언제 (when) & N에 (at/on)　　　p. 119

A　1. 저녁　　　　　　　2. 밤
　　3. 아침　　　　　　　4. 오후

B　1. 오후에　　　　　　2. 아침에 (or 오전에)
　　3. 밤에　　　　　　　4. 낮에

C　1. 아침(or 오전) 여덟 시　　2. 아침(or 오전) 아홉 시
　　3. 오후 세 시　　　　　　4. 저녁 여섯 시

Unit 4　Asking and Telling Dates　　　p. 121

A　1. 이천십삼년　　　　　2. 천칠백팔십년
　　3. 천구백구십오년　　　4. 이천육년

B　1. 유월 십구일　　　　　2. 십이월 이십육일
　　3. 시월 육일　　　　　　4. 오월 삼십일일

C　1. 토요일이에요.　　2. 팔월 십이일이에요.

3. 수요일이에요.　　4. (팔월) 이십구일에 (한국에) 가요.

Unit 5　N부터 N까지 (from N to N)　　　p. 123

A　1. 부터　　　　　　　2. 부터, 까지
　　3. 까지　　　　　　　4. 부터

B　1. 에서　　　　　　　2. 부터
　　3. 부터　　　　　　　4. 에서

C　1. 부터, 까지, 두 시부터 네 시까지
　　2. 까지, 여덟 시까지
　　3. 부터, 일월 일일부터
　　4. 까지, 일요일까지

REVIEW TEST　　　p. 126

A　③ 병 for cups (→ 잔 for cups, 병 for bottles)

B　② 이천이십삼년 팔월 이십삼일

C　③ 열 시 십 분 전 (→ 열한 시 십 분 전)

D　④ 몇 시 - 무슨 요일

E　② 책 한 분 (→ 책 한 권)

F　④ 언제부터 한국어를 배워요?

G　③ 민호는 칠월 오일까지 서울에 있습니다.
　　(→ 민호는 칠월 오일부터 서울에 있습니다.)

VOCABULARY　　　p. 127

1. to take (time)　　　　2. dog

3. store, shop　　　　　4. England

5. movie　　　　　　　6. class, lesson

7. exam, test　　　　　8. time, hour

9. part time job　　　　10. Seoul

11. Busan　　　　　　12. tomorrow

13. however, by the way

Chapter 9　Basic Particles

Unit 1　N와/과, N(이)랑, N하고 (and/with)　　　p. 131

A　1. 과, 이랑　　　　　　2. 와, 랑

3. 와, 랑   4. 과, 이랑

B 1. 독일과 프랑스 / 독일이랑 프랑스 / 독일하고 프랑스
   2. 요리와 운동 / 요리랑 운동 / 요리하고 운동
   3. 가방과 핸드폰 / 가방이랑 핸드폰 / 가방하고 핸드폰
   4. 책과 연필 / 책이랑 연필 / 책하고 연필

C 1. 와 같이 (or 함께)   2.하고 같이 (or 함께)
   3. 과 같이 (or 함께)   4. 이랑 같이 (or 함께)

Unit 2 N이나, N 아니면 N (or)   p. 133

A 1. 나   2. 나
   3. 이나   4. 나

B 1. 나   2. 나
   3. 이나   4. 나, 이나

C 1. 저는 보통 콜라 아니면 주스를 마셔요.
   2. 월요일 아니면 화요일에 병원에 가요.
   3. 오빠가 버스 아니면 자전거를 타요.
   4. 내일 아니면 주말에 여자친구를 만나요.

Unit 3 N도 (also), N만 (only)   p. 135

A 1. 도   2. 도
   3. 에도   4. 에서도

B 1. 에서만   2. 만
   3. 에만   4. 만

C 1. 떡볶이도   2. 오빠만
   3. 미국에서만   4. 밤에도

Unit 4 N에게/N한테 (to)   p. 137

A 1. 에게   2. 에
   3. 에   4. 에게

B 1. 에   2. 에게
   3. 에게서(or 에게)   4. 에게

C 1. 한테, 엄마한테 말해요.
   2. 에게, 친구에게 이메일을 보내요.
   3. 에게, 토미에게 한국어를 배워요.
   4. 에게, 여동생에게 가요.

Unit 5 N(으)로 (to/with)   p. 139

A 1. 로   2. 으로

3. 으로   4. 로

B 1. 으로   2. 로
   3. 으로   4. 로

C 1. A   2. B
   3. B   4. A

REVIEW TEST   p. 142

A ② 와 - 과

B ③ 저는 비빔밥랑 김치를 먹어요.
   (→ 저는 비빔밥이랑 김치를 먹어요.)

C ① 엄마가 영화를 봐요. 아빠도 영화를 봐요.

D ③ 핸드폰만으로 (→ 핸드폰으로만)

E ③ 저는 매일 꽃에게 물을 줘요. (→ 꽃에)

F ④ 바다 - 핸드폰

G ② 유코는 일요일에만 일찍 일어납니다.
   (→ 유코는 일요일에만 일찍 안 일어납니다.)

VOCABULARY   p. 143

1. to wait   2. to make
3. to receive   4. to send
5. to know   6. to sell
7. to talk   8. to travel
9. to call   10. puppy, dog
11. train   12. bus
13. airplane   14. department store
15. kitchen   16. birthday
17. present, gift   18. English
19. email   20. letter
21. juice   22. kimchi
23. tteokbokki   24. ramyeon
25. bibimbap   26. right side
27. left side   28. normally
29. very   30. usually
31. weekend

Chapter 10 Describing Traits

Unit 1 Adjectives & 어떻다 (to be how)   p. 147

A 1. 따뜻해요   2. 비싸요
     3. 맛있어요   4. 길어요

B 1. 맛있어요.   2. 싸요.
     3. 작아요.   4. 좋아요.

C 1. 어때요   2. 어때요
     3. 어떻습니까   4. 어때

Unit 2 N보다 (than), 더 (more), 덜 (less)   p. 149

A 1. 주스보다 더 시원해요.   2. 부산보다 덜 따뜻해요.
     3. 자동차보다 더 길어요.   4. 빵보다 덜 맛있어요.

B 1. 핸드폰이 컴퓨터보다   2. 드라마를 영화보다
     3. 엄마가 아빠보다   4. 주스를 커피보다

C 1. 영미가 지수보다 더 작아요.
     2. 목요일이 수요일보다 더 따뜻요.
     3. 모자가 치마보다 더 싸요.
     4. 병원이 학교보다 더 멀어요.

Unit 3 가장/제일 (the most), N 중에서 (among)   p. 151

A 1. 김치가 가장 (or 제일) 맛있어요.
     2. 오늘 날씨가 가장 (or 제일) 좋아요.
     3. 기차가 가장 (or 제일) 길어요.
     4. 저는 한국어를 가장 (or 제일) 자주 말해요.

B 1. 중에서   2. 중에서
     3. 에서   4. 에서

C 1. 제 친구 중에서   2. 한국에서
     3. 핸드폰 중에서   4. 회사에서

Unit 4 무슨, 어떤, 어느 (what, which)   p. 153

A 1. 어떤   2. 어느
     3. 무슨   4. 어느

B 1. 무슨   2. 무슨
     3. 어떤   4. 어느

C 1. 판타지 영화를 싫어해요.   2. 라면이 맛있어요.
     3. (친구랑) 한국을 여행해요.   4. 바나나를 제일 좋아해요.

REVIEW TEST   p. 156

A ③ 멀다 - 멀어요

B ④ 요즘 한국 드라마보다 제일 재미있어요.
     (→ 요즘 한국 드라마가 제일 재미있어요.)

C ① 좋어요 (→ 좋아요)

D ③ 회사 중에서 (→ 회사에서)

E ② 저는 한국 음식 중에서 라면을 제일 좋아해요.

F ① 무슨 - 어느

G ④ 민호는 과일을 먹지 않습니다.
     (→ 민호는 요즘 과일만 먹습니다.)

VOCABULARY   p. 157

1. to be long   2. to be high
3. to be warm   4. to be delicious
5. to be far   6. to be cool, to be stylish
7. to be expensive   8. to be cool
9. to be cheap   10. to be small
11. to be fun   12. to be good
13. to be cloudy   14. to not like
15. fruit   16. food
17. ice cream   18. country
19. weather   20. Jeju island
21. well   22. really
23. a litte

Chapter 11 Irregular Conjugations

Unit 1 '—' Conjugations   p. 161

A 1. 아이가 정말 예뻐요.
     2. 선생님에게 이메일을 써요.
     3. 마리아가 요즘 너무 바빠요.
     4. 오늘 날씨가 조금 나빠요.

B 1. 아파요.   2. 써요.
     3. 슬퍼요.   4. 커요.

C 1. 바빠요.   2. 나빠요.
   3. 슬퍼요.   4. 아파요.

Unit 2 'ㅂ' Conjugations   p. 163

A 1. 추워요   2. 도와요
   3. 입어요   4. 매워요

B 1. 가벼워요.   2. 매워요.
   3. 입어요.   4. 쉬워요.

C 1. 귀여워요.   2. 더워요.
   3. 도와요.   4. 추워요.

Unit 3 'ㄷ' Conjugations   p. 165

A 1. 받아요   2. 들어요
   3. 닫아요   4. 물어요

B 1. 닫아요.   2. 걸어요.
   3. 받아요.   4. 물어요.

C 1. 걸어요.   2. 받아요.
   3. 물어요.   4. 들어요.

Unit 4 'ㄹ' Conjugations   p. 167

A 1. 불러요   2. 몰라요
   3. 달라요   4. 골라요

B 1. 골라요?.   2. 몰라요.
   3. 빨라요.   4. 불러요.

C 1. 불러요.   2. 달라요.
   3. 골라요.   4. 몰라요.

REVIEW TEST   p. 170

A ① 나쁘다 - 나뻐요 (→ 나빠요)

B ③ 불러요 - 골라요

C ④ 우리 집은 너무 좁아요.

D ③ 받다

E ① 바쁘어요 (→ 바빠요)

F ③ 서울이랑 부산 중에 어디가 더 덥어요? (→ 더워요?)

G ③ 가방이 제니에게 예쁩니다.
     (→ 가방이 제니에게 귀엽습니다.)

VOCABULARY   p. 171

1. to be light	2. to be cute
3. to be bad	4. to be different
5. to be hot	6. to be spicy
7. to be heavy	8. to be busy
9. to be fast	10. to be easy
11. to be sad	12. to be sick
13. to be difficult	14. to be pretty
15. to be narrow	16. to be cold
17. to be big	18. to walk
19. to choose	20. to close
21. to help	22. to hear, to listen (to)
23. to not know	24. to ask
25. to sing, to call	26. to write
27. to wear	28. road, street
29. head	30. music
31. height	32. too, so
33. a lot, much	34. however, but

Index of Grammar

Index of Vocabulary

ㄱ

가게	store, shop	Ch. 8
가다	to go	Ch. 6
가르치다	to teach	Ch. 6
가방	bag	Ch. 3
가볍다	to be light	Ch. 11
가수	singer	Ch. 2
가장	the most	Ch. 10
가족	family	Ch. 5
감사	appreciation	Ch. 1
강아지	puppy	Ch. 9
같이	together	Ch. 9
개1	dog	Ch. 8
개2	counter for things	Ch. 8
거기	there	Ch. 4
거실	living room	Ch. 4
걷다	to walk	Ch. 11
걸리다	to take (time)	Ch. 8
고기	meat	Ch. 7
고르다	to choose	Ch. 11
고맙다	to be grateful	Ch. 1
고양이	cat	Ch. 4
공부하다	to study	Ch. 6
공원	park	Ch. 4
공책	notebook	Ch. 3
과일	fruit	Ch. 10
교실	classroom	Ch. 4
구	nine	Ch. 1
구십	ninety	Ch. 1
구월	september	Ch. 8
권	counter for books	Ch. 8
귀엽다	to be cute	Ch. 11
그	that	Ch. 3

그것	that thing, that	Ch. 3
그래서	so, therefore	Ch. 7
그런데	however, by the way	Ch. 8
그럼	then	Ch. 5
그리고	and	Ch. 4
그림	picture, painting	Ch. 3
금요일	Friday	Ch. 8
기다리다	to wait	Ch. 9
기차	train	Ch. 9
길	road, street	Ch. 11
길다	to be long	Ch. 10
김치	Kimchi	Ch. 9
꽃	flower	Ch. 3

ㄴ

나	I (casual)	Ch. 2
나라	country	Ch. 10
나무	tree	Ch. 3
나쁘다	to be bad	Ch. 11
날씨	weather	Ch. 10
남동생	older brother	Ch. 2
남산	Nam mountain	Ch. 3
남자	man	Ch. 5
남편	husband	Ch. 5
낮	day, daytime	Ch. 8
내	my (casual)	Ch. 5
내일	tomorrow	Ch. 8
너	you (casual)	Ch. 5
너무	too, so	Ch. 11
네	yes (polite)	Ch. 2
네	your (polite)	Ch. 8
넷	four	Ch. 1
년	year	Ch. 8

노래하다	to song	Ch. 7
높다	to be high	Ch. 10
누구	who	Ch. 5
누나	older sister for boys	Ch. 2
님	(honorific title)	Ch. 2

ㄷ

다르다	to be different	Ch. 11
다섯	five	Ch. 1
닫다	to close	Ch. 11
대학생	college student	Ch. 2
더	more	Ch. 10
덥다	to be hot	Ch. 11
도서관	library	Ch. 4
독일	Germany	Ch. 2
돕다	to help	Ch. 11
동생	younger brother/sister	Ch. 2
두	two	Ch. 8
둘	two	Ch. 1
뒤	behind	Ch. 4
드라마	drama	Ch. 6
듣다	to hear	Ch. 11
따뜻하다	to be warm	Ch. 10
딸	daughter	Ch. 5
떡볶이	Tteokbokki	Ch. 9

ㄹ

라면	Ramyeon	Ch. 9

ㅁ

마리	counter for animals	Ch. 8
마시다	to drink	Ch. 6
마흔	forty	Ch. 1
만	ten thousand	Ch. 9
만나다	to meet	Ch. 6

만들다	to make	Ch. 9
많이	a lot, much	Ch. 11
말하다	to talk	Ch. 9
맛있다	to be delicious	Ch. 10
매일	every day	Ch. 7
맵다	to be spicy	Ch. 11
머리	head	Ch. 11
먹다	to eat	Ch. 6
멀다	to be far	Ch. 10
멋있다	to be cool, to be stylish	Ch. 10
며칠	what date	Ch. 8
명	counter for people	Ch. 8
몇	how many	Ch. 8
모르다	to not know	Ch. 11
모자	hat	Ch. 3
목요일	Thursday	Ch. 8
못	not (can)	Ch. 7
무겁다	to be heavy	Ch. 11
무슨	which	Ch. 10
무엇	what	Ch. 3
묻다	to ask	Ch. 11
물	water	Ch. 7
뭐	what (abb.)	Ch. 3
미국	USA	Ch. 2
미안하다	to be sorry	Ch. 1
밑	under	Ch. 4

ㅂ

바나나	banana	Ch. 7
바다	sea	Ch. 4
바쁘다	to be busy	Ch. 11
밖	outside	Ch. 4
반갑다	to be glad	Ch. 2
받다	to receive	Ch. 9
밤	night, night time	Ch. 8

밥	rice	Ch. 6
방	room	Ch. 4
배우	actor	Ch. 2
배우다	to learn	Ch. 6
백	hundred	Ch. 1
백화점	department store	Ch. 9
버스	bus	Ch. 9
병	bottle	Ch. 8
병원	hospital	Ch. 4
보내다	to send	Ch. 9
보다	to see, to watch	Ch. 6
보다	than	Ch. 10
보통	normally	Ch. 9
부르다	to sing, to call	Ch. 11
부모님	parents	Ch. 5
부산	Busan	Ch. 8
부엌	kitchen	Ch. 9
분	person (honorifics)	Ch. 5
분	counter for people	Ch. 8
분	minute	Ch. 8
비빔밥	Bibimbap	Ch. 9
비싸다	to be expensive	Ch. 10
비행기	airplane	Ch. 9
빠르다	to be fast	Ch. 11
빵	bread	Ch. 6

ㅅ

사	four	Ch. 1
사과	apple	Ch. 7
사다	to buy	Ch. 7
사람	person	Ch. 2
사랑하다	to love	Ch. 6
사십	forty	Ch. 1
사월	April	Ch. 8
사이	between	Ch. 4

사장님	boss, CEO	Ch. 5
사진	picture, photo	Ch. 5
산	mountain	Ch. 4
살	counter for age	Ch. 8
살다	to live	Ch. 6
삼	three	Ch. 10
삼십	thirty	Ch. 10
삼월	March	Ch. 8
상자	box	Ch. 4
생일	birthday	Ch. 9
샤워하다	to take a shower	Ch. 7
서른	thirty	Ch. 1
서울	Seoul	Ch. 8
서점	bookstore	Ch. 4
선물	gift	Ch. 9
선생님	teacher	Ch. 2
세	three	Ch. 8
셋	three	Ch. 1
손	hand	Ch. 7
쇼핑	shopping	Ch. 5
수업	class, lesson	Ch. 8
수영	swimming	Ch. 5
수요일	Wednesday	Ch. 8
술	drink, alcohol	Ch. 7
쉬다	to rest	Ch. 6
쉽다	to be easy	Ch. 11
스물	twenty	Ch. 1
슬프다	to be sad	Ch. 11
시	hours	Ch. 8
시간	time, hour	Ch. 8
시원하다	to be cool	Ch. 10
시월	October	Ch. 8
시험	exam, test	Ch. 8
식당	restaurant	Ch. 4
신발	shoes	Ch. 3

싫어하다	to not like	Ch. 10
십	ten	Ch. 1
십이월	December	Ch. 8
십일월	November	Ch. 8
싸다	to be cheap	Ch. 10
쓰다	to write	Ch. 11
씨	Mr., Mrs.	Ch. 2
씻다	to wash	Ch. 7

ㅇ

아기	baby	Ch. 5
아내	wife	Ch. 5
아니다	to not be	Ch. 2
아니요	no (polite)	Ch. 2
아들	son	Ch. 5
아래	under	Ch. 4
아르바이트	part time job	Ch. 8
아버지	father	Ch. 2
아빠	dad	Ch. 2
아이	child	Ch. 3
아이스크림	ice cream	Ch. 10
아주	very	Ch. 9
아침	morning	Ch. 8
아프다	to be sick	Ch. 11
아홉	nine	Ch. 1
아흔	ninety	Ch. 1
안	inside	Ch. 4
안	not (do)	Ch. 7
안경	glasses	Ch. 5
안녕	peace	Ch. 2
안녕히	in peace	Ch. 1
앉다	to sit	Ch. 6
알다	to know	Ch. 9
앞	front	Ch. 4
어느	which	Ch. 10

어디	where	Ch. 4
어떤	what kind of	Ch. 10
어렵다	to be difficult	Ch. 11
어머니	mother	Ch. 2
언니	older sister for girls	Ch. 2
언제	when	Ch. 8
엄마	mom	Ch. 2
없다	to not exist	Ch. 4
여기	here	Ch. 4
여덟	eight	Ch. 1
여동생	younger sister	Ch. 2
여든	eighty	Ch. 1
여섯	six	Ch. 1
여자	woman	Ch. 5
여행하다	to travel	Ch. 9
연필	pencil	Ch. 3
열다	to open	Ch. 7
영	zero	Ch. 1
영국	England	Ch. 8
영어	English	Ch. 9
영화	movie	Ch. 8
영화배우	movie actor	Ch. 5
옆	next	Ch. 4
예	yes (polite)	Ch. 2
예쁘다	to be pretty	Ch. 11
오	five	Ch. 1
오늘	today	Ch. 7
오다	to come	Ch. 6
오른쪽	right side	Ch. 9
오빠	older brother for girls	Ch. 2
오십	fifty	Ch. 1
오월	May	Ch. 8
오전	morning	Ch. 8
오후	afternoon	Ch. 8
옷	clothes	Ch. 3

왼쪽	left side	Ch. 9	일흔	seventy	Ch. 1
요리하다	to cook	Ch. 6	읽다	to read	Ch. 6
요일	day of the week	Ch. 8	입다	to wear	Ch. 11
요즘	these days	Ch. 7	있다	to exist	Ch. 4
우리	we (casual)	Ch. 5			
우산	umbrella	Ch. 3	**ㅈ**		
우유	milk	Ch. 7	자다	to sleep	Ch. 6
운동하다	to exercise	Ch. 6	자동차	car	Ch. 3
운전하다	to drive	Ch. 7	자전거	bike	Ch. 7
월	month	Ch. 8	자주	often	Ch. 7
월요일	Monday	Ch. 8	작다	to be small	Ch. 10
위	top	Ch. 4	잔	glass	Ch. 8
유월	June	Ch. 8	잘	well	Ch. 10
육	six	Ch. 1	재미있다	to be fun	Ch. 10
육십	sixty	Ch. 1	저	I (polite)	Ch. 2
은행	bank	Ch. 4	저	that	Ch. 3
음식	meal	Ch. 10	저것	that thing, that	Ch. 3
음악	music	Ch. 11	저기	there	Ch. 4
의사	doctor	Ch. 2	저녁	evening	Ch. 8
의자	chair	Ch. 4	전화하다	to call	Ch. 9
이	two	Ch. 1	점심	lunch	Ch. 8
이	this	Ch. 3	정말	really	Ch. 10
이것	this thing, this	Ch. 3	제	my (polite)	Ch. 3
이름	name	Ch. 5	제일	the most	Ch. 10
이메일	email	Ch. 9	제주도	Jeju island	Ch. 10
이십	twenty	Ch. 1	조금	a litte	Ch. 10
이월	February	Ch. 8	좁다	to be narrow	Ch. 11
일	one	Ch. 1	좋다	to be good	Ch. 10
일	day	Ch. 8	좋아하다	to like	Ch. 6
일곱	seven	Ch. 1	죄송하다	to be sorry	Ch. 1
일어나다	to get up	Ch. 7	주다	to give	Ch. 6
일요일	Sunday	Ch. 8	주로	usually	Ch. 9
일월	January	Ch. 8	주말	weekend	Ch. 9
일찍	early	Ch. 7	주스	juice	Ch. 9
일하다	to work	Ch. 6	중국	China	Ch. 5

지금	now	Ch. 7
직업	oppupation, job	Ch. 5
집	house	Ch. 4

ㅊ		
창문	window	Ch. 4
책	book	Ch. 3
책상	desk	Ch. 4
청소하다	to clean up	Ch. 7
춥다	to be cold	Ch. 11
취미	hobby	Ch. 5
치마	skirt	Ch. 3
친구	friend	Ch. 3
칠	seven	Ch. 1
칠십	seventy	Ch. 1
칠월	July	Ch. 8
칠판	black board	Ch. 4
침대	bed	Ch. 4

ㅋ		
카메라	camera	Ch. 3
카페	cafe	Ch. 4
커피	coffee	Ch. 7
커피숍	coffee shop	Ch. 4
컴퓨터	computer	Ch. 3
컵	cup	Ch. 4
콜라	cola	Ch. 6
크다	to be big	Ch. 11
키	height	Ch. 11

ㅌ		
타다	to ride	Ch. 6
텔레비전	television	Ch. 3
토요일	Saturday	Ch. 8

ㅍ		
파티	party	Ch. 7
팔	eight	Ch. 1
팔다	to sell	Ch. 9
팔십	eighty	Ch. 1
팔월	August	Ch. 8
편지	letter	Ch. 9
프랑스	France	Ch. 5
피아노	piano	Ch. 4

ㅎ		
하나	one	Ch. 1
하다	to do	Ch. 6
하지만	but, however	Ch. 11
학교	school	Ch. 4
학생	student	Ch. 2
한	one	Ch. 8
한국	Korea	Ch. 2
한국어	Korean (language)	Ch. 3
할머니	grandmother	Ch. 3
할아버지	grandfather	Ch. 3
함께	together	Ch. 9
핸드폰	cellphone	Ch. 3
형	older brother for boys	Ch. 2
화요일	Tuesday	Ch. 8
회사	company	Ch. 5
회사원	office worker	Ch. 2
흐리다	to be cloudy	Ch. 10

About the Author

Tomi (Lee Insuk):

Tomi was born and raised in Seoul, South Korea, and currently resides in Germany. In Korea, she studied Korean history at Sungkyunkwan University, the oldest university in Korea. Working as an editor for the Korean cultural magazine <PAPER>, she also engaged in scriptwriting for Korean broadcasters such as MBC and MTV.

After immigrating to Germany, Tomi began teaching Korean to foreign students. For several years, she worked as a Korean language teacher at the Bremen Korean School and Inlingua language school. With a dream of making Korean language learning easier and more enjoyable for learners worldwide, she actively participates on Instagram.

Instagram: @tomikorean
YouTube Channel: @tomikoren

Contributors to Production:
Text: Byun Stella Jiyoung, Hwang Bora
Design: Suh Yunda
English Review: Ryu Soohyun
Media: Jung Sanghoon

Your Opinion Counts!

We sincerely hope this book has been a helpful companion in your Korean language learning.

If you find this book helpful, please take a moment to leave a review on our website and help other Korean learners discover it.
We kindly ask for your review!

Thank you so much!